REPRODUCING REVOLUTION

REPRODUCING REVOLUTION

Women's Labor and the War
in Kachinland

Jenny Hedström

SOUTHEAST ASIA PROGRAM PUBLICATIONS

AN IMPRINT OF CORNELL UNIVERSITY PRESS   ITHACA AND LONDON

Thanks to generous funding from the Swedish Defense University, the ebook editions of this book are available as open access volumes through the Cornell Open initiative.

First published 2025 by Cornell University Press

Library of Congress Cataloging-in-Publication Data

Names: Hedström, Jenny, author.
Title: Reproducing revolution : women's labor and the war in Kachinland / Jenny Hedström.
Description: Ithaca : Southeast Asia Program Publications, an imprint of Cornell University Press, 2025. | Includes bibliographical references and index.
Identifiers: LCCN 2024054356 (print) | LCCN 2024054357 (ebook) | ISBN 9781501782541 (hardcover) | ISBN 9781501782558 (paperback) | ISBN 9781501782572 (epub) | ISBN 9781501782565 (pdf)
Subjects: LCSH: Women in war—Burma—Kachin State. | Home economics—Social aspects—Burma—Kachin State. | Women—Burma—Kachin State—Social conditions.
Classification: LCC HQ666.7.Z9 .K33 2025 (print) | LCC HQ666.7.Z9 (ebook) | DDC 959.105/4—dc23/eng/20250120
LC record available at https://lccn.loc.gov/2024054356
LC ebook record available at https://lccn.loc.gov/2024054357

Contents

Preface

The woman sitting before me, Seng Rai, has steel-black hair drawn back into a tight bun. One lock has escaped and curls, unruly, around her cheekbone. Her younger friend, whose name I do not quite catch, sips at her tea; she mostly nods in agreement while Seng Rai speaks. They came to this interview together, wearing matching Mickey Mouse pajama bottoms. The translator and I are in a displaced persons' camp in rural Kachinland to interview women about their sense of security in the camps and their experiences of war. The smiling face of Mickey Mouse seems to wink at me when Seng Rai moves her legs, adding a sense of absurdity to the situation.

Seng Rai and her friend talk about cattle for what feels like a very long time. The room is hot, I am tired, and my mind, regrettably, begins to wander. Suddenly I tense up, sensing that something is about to happen, and then it does: Seng Rai breaks down, hitting her head with her hands, saying she wants it empty. She says she cannot stop hearing bullets. The younger woman pats the arm of her friend, and I look at my translator for guidance. She is quiet and looks pale. Unnerved, I turn off the recorder. I ask what we can do for Seng Rai—maybe counseling with the local women's group active in the camp, I suggest, or a referral somewhere outside—but her friend shakes her head and pats Seng Rai again. She even pats me on my arm as they turn to leave, as if I am the one needing comforting.

I realize afterward that perhaps the reason Seng Rai talked so much about her cattle is because she cannot talk about her other losses. She has lived through three violent cycles of the war; in addition to losing her cattle and her land, she also lost her husband and two of her children. The first time she was attacked by the Myanmar armed forces was in the 1980s. The second time was in 1993. She had been shot at from helicopters as she fled the war with her youngest child in a basket on her back. When the area she lived in experienced attacks in June 2011, she had to relocate to a displaced persons' camp for the third time in her life.

In interview after interview, I hear similar stories: women hiding in fields, children lifted into baskets, some too stunned to cry. After a while, these wars collapse into one another. When the Myanmar soldiers come, there is only this. This is one moment and many; one war and many. Time repeats itself.

Over the course of this research, I have heard many brutal stories—and just as many telling silences. A sharp intake of breath, a sudden flutter of hands, words straining to get out. War has a way of lingering in bodies, of creating silences so thick you think you cannot reach through them.

Yet what strikes me most about the women who spoke to me is the way that they *keep going*, in spite of what they have lived through. Seng Rai's temporary breakdown was an anomaly in my interviews, shedding light on a usually concealed abyss of pain. Women in Kachinland must find ways to keep doing what is necessary for their families' survival and the war effort despite the exhaustion and trauma their bodies have sustained. They must keep going—because if they stop, the revolution would grind to a halt.

In this book, I draw attention to the often-overlooked subject of women's labor and how it sustains military efforts in Kachinland. Women in Kachin households shoulder a huge responsibility in ensuring the survival of their communities through cycles of intractable conflict. Dominant accounts of the Kachin war(s) are preoccupied with the conduct of the state or the actions of military leaders; to my knowledge, the literature on conflict does little to analyze everyday women's labor in revolutionary warfare, deeming it not important enough for serious assessment. Women do fight alongside men, and their experiences as soldiers are instructive and important. Yet focusing on female soldiers alone does not go far enough: the household is an integral, if often overlooked, unit in the Kachin military project. It is women's household labor that replenishes families and soldiers and, at the same time, reproduces gendered hierarchies and labor. This is work that is risky; it requires both courage and creativity.

This book proposes that both longevity and insecurity in conflict must be understood in relationship to the division and devaluation of women's reproductive and productive labor. It suggests that the household is a critical, if overlooked, site from where war is felt and reproduced. A focus on the household might therefore explain one of the most puzzling aspects of the ongoing Kachin war given the logistical and practical superiority of the Myanmar military—its perseverance. The Kachin armed forces should be no match for the Myanmar armed forces, by many accounts estimated to be at least ten times the size of the Kachin Independence Organisation (KIO) and the Kachin Independence Army (KIA). Yet the KIO does mount a formidable defense, year after year. How is this possible?

Much ink has been spilled analyzing the reasons for the war and its stubborn continuation. Some say ethnic identity or religious belonging can explain the war and its persistence. Others point to the power of drugs, the lack of stable institutions, or the influence of colonialism on the uptake of arms. Still others look at intragroup relationships, arguing that the internal dynamics of the Kachin armed group or the state military can help explain why and how the wars continue across generations. These are all important interventions that my book builds on and extends from.[1] Yet the gendered dynamics of the Kachin armed movement are largely overlooked.

In this book, I argue that the replenishment of the military household, in Kachin as well as elsewhere, is critical for military labor power, which women help realize through (cheap) gendered labor centered on the household, or what I call militarized social reproduction.

This means that I understand women's social reproductive and productive duties as underpinning not only the market by reproducing labor power (Federici 2004, 2019) but broader war economies too (Peterson 2009), extending on theories of social reproduction that tend to focus on the household in relation to factories or farms, not revolutions and wars. To paraphrase Nancy Fraser, these are activities that produce and maintain household and military bonds through taken-for-granted and often invisible labor (Fraser 2017, 23). The following chapters explore how women activists in the Kachin Women's Association (KWA), female soldiers in the Kachin Independence Army (KIA), and wives and widows living in army brigades and in internally displaced persons' camps labor to make ends meet and provide for their families and the broader revolution through vital but often underpaid or unpaid work. Inspired both by the women I met and learned from and feminist scholarship on political economy (Bhattacharya 2017; Chisholm 2022; Federici 2004; Mies 2014; True 2012), war (Enloe 2000; Nordstrom 1997; Sylvester 2012), and the everyday (Scheper-Hughes 1992; Smith 1987), I propose that paying attention to women's labor reveals both war's violence and its reproduction, emphasizing how women at different points in their lives—from soldiers to widows—negotiate, resist, and/or uphold broader relations of military power and might through social reproductive and productive labor.

This book insists that women are revolutionary subjects. Their everyday practices sustain communities besieged by war. This is not to say that all women do this work all the time or that this work always stays the same. As Lila Abu-Lughod (1993) reminds us, no relationship is static. But by looking at the particular, we might learn something about the general, which is another way of saying that scholars of war and politics should pay careful attention to the everyday interactions and relationships that shape violence and its devastating effects.

According to the literature on women in armed rebellions and nationalistic movements, women's inclusion in military organizations does not upset gender hierarchies as much as it reinforces them, at least in the postwar period when any possible gains for women's rights tend to be further marginalized (see Peterson 2010; Alison 2009; Yuval-Davis 1997; Cockburn 2010). We know from previous work exploring gender and upheaval in Myanmar that women have always been an integral part of struggles for independence, nationalism or democracy: sometimes as frontline leaders (Elliot 1999; Lintner 1990, 2000), soldiers (Ferguson

2013; Lebra 2008; Tharaphi Than 2014), and village heads (The Karen Women's Organization 2010; Zin Mar Oo and Kusakabe 2010), and other times as community organizers, nurses, and educators (Harriden 2012; Saw Ralph and Naw Sheera 2020; Thawnghmung and Cho 2013). Yet it seems that their sacrifices have not been given the same value and recognition as men's. What women's involvement in the Kachin military project means, legally and politically, for any possible transformations of gender hierarchies is too early to know. As the anthropologist Saba Mahmood reminds us, revolutions are always contingent and must therefore be understood from within specific subjective and emplaced struggles. In light of this, attention to women's participation in the Kachin struggles can help us reimagine how we understand and theorize nationalistic projects, not least by moving away from simplistic portrayals as either victims or agendas of war (Mahmood 2005).

The focus on the everyday household labor and conduct of women living in the territory controlled by the Kachin armed forces rather than on the heads of armies and the behavior of states shows how empirically grounded research is critical for developing new theoretical insights into the conduct and outbreak of war. By allowing us to see beyond soldiers, strategies, and statistics, a focus on women's everyday labor—or what I call militarized social reproduction—helps us ask different questions about wars, their effects and their endurance. This task is more urgent than ever. As I am writing these notes, in 2024, the Myanmar junta's brutal counterinsurgency campaigns are intensifying: in the aftermath of the 2021 military coup, the UN has found evidence of "a dramatic increase in war crimes" (UN Human Rights Council 2023). In Kachinland, the blockage of aid to displaced communities means that thousands of families are going hungry.[2] In wars such as those fought in Myanmar, where the state's counterinsurgency measures are aimed at obliterating ethnic minority communities, literally rupturing ties to culture, kin, and nation, women's labor in maintaining and forging ties to home and community remains a fundamental but often overlooked site of resistance and endurance.

The findings of this book are heavily based on primary sources, including over a hundred interviews with female soldiers, students, and residents in displaced persons' camps, male political leaders, male foot soldiers, and women's rights activists, collected across a ten-year period from 2013 to 2023. It uses rich empirical source material to examine the Kachin revolution and to illustrate the importance of women's experiences for understanding the war. These people's knowledge and experiences have ultimately allowed me to examine the complex mixture of women's agency and structural inequality that goes into sustaining the resistance efforts of this particular war. They have taught me about the commitment of women to keep their families and communities alive despite, or because of, the entrenched violence of the Myanmar state.

Acknowledgments

This book has taken a long time to write, and I am grateful to people all across the world who have helped this book see the light of day. Research is no singular undertaking—even if it is my name on the cover—and the following people have contributed in many different ways. Mistakes, however, are my own.

Starting in Thailand, thank you to my sisters at the Burmese Women's Union, who first provided a place for me to stay and an opportunity to learn about women in Myanmar. I am particularly grateful to Mi Sue Pwint, Khin Ohmar, Tin Tin Nyo, Ma Hnoung, Htwe Htwe, and Eh Wah for teaching me about their lives and about the broader movement for rights in Burma. Special thanks must of course be extended to Zin Mar Phyo, Thwel Zin Phyo, and Ei Mon Phyo for the many laughs, dresses, and meals that have sustained me over the years. I am also very grateful to the women at the Kachin Women's Association Thailand, who initially taught me about the Kachin armed struggle: Shirley Seng, Jessica, Mary, Moon Nay Li, and Julia Marip who, alongside Ja Htoi Pan Maran and Stella Naw, patiently shared with me their intimate knowledge of Kachinland.

The people involved with the Kachinland Research Centre, the Humanity Institute and the Kachin Women's Association have in different ways assisted with my research and enriched my knowledge. While in Thailand, Amy and Matthew Smith have not only provided a roof over my head but have also acted as role models for the kind of engaged researcher I should be. I miss Ma Wat Smith, whose heartfelt and enthusiastic greetings always made my Bangkok "home" feel truly like home. I am grateful to David Baulk, who read and commented on my PhD work, even when under tight deadlines himself. Spanning Myanmar and Thailand, special thanks must also be given to my fellow feminist sisters: Melanie Walker for laughs, a good balcony, and beers; Alicia de la Cour Venning, travel partner and research collaborator extraordinaire; and Annami Löfving, for her feminist curiosity, much-needed irreverence, and (possibly life-saving) tahini. I value my friendship with Kay (Valentina) Soe, who always made time to chat, eat together, and teach me about what matters. I also want to thank Bertil Lintner and Mandy Sadan, who both have shared their immense knowledge of Myanmar, and of Kachin state, with me.

In Australia, my PhD supervisors, Professor Jacqui True, Dr. Samanthi Gunawardana, and Dr. Swati Parashar, have all provided thoughtful guidance, advice, and feedback. I have benefited immensely from their vast competence in the field. I extend special thanks to Swati and Ravi (Swati's spouse), who kindly provided my husband and I with a warm place to stay when we first arrived in Australia. Thanks also to Swati's mother Uma for sustaining us with her excellent cooking during those early weeks. We still dream of her curries.

My fellow PhD students and colleagues at Monash Gender, Peace and Security Centre were a source of inspiration and encouragement. In particular, I want to thank Kate Lee-Koo and Lesley Pruitt, as well as Yasmin Chilmeran (and Fred!), Sarah Hewitt, Sara Phillips, Maria Tanyag, and Barbara Trojanowska. I am indebted to Sue Stevenson for her extensive and in-depth knowledge of all things related to administrative matters, and to Professor Ann Tickner. Of course, my office environment would not have been half as pleasant without the company of Dara Conduit, Stephanie Carver, and Samantha Kruber.

Research for the thesis was initially carried out in Myanmar and Thailand with generous financial support from Monash Graduate Scholarship, Monash International Postgraduate Scholarship, and funding from Karl Staff Fond, for which I am very grateful. Funding that helped me turn the thesis into book came from the Swedish Research Council.

In Sweden I want to thank my fellow colleagues in the Gender, Peace and Security working group who read drafts, drank coffee, and made work so much more fun: Annick Wibben, Elin Berg, Emma Fredriksson, Priscyll Anctil Avoine, Leena Vastapuu, Mariam Bjarnesen, Moa Peldán, July Decarpentrie, and of course Elisabeth Olivius, honorary GPS member. I also owe a great debt of gratitude to my scattered Burma studies crowd—Khin Khin Mra, Tomas Cole, Elizabeth Rhoades, Justine Chambers, Courtney Wittekind, Hilary Faxon, Laur Kiik, David Brenner, and Nick Cheesman—who have all in their own way made this multiyear research endeavor much more inspired and enjoyable. Many have commented on chapter drafts, talked me through outlines, and commiserated with me, while out running or over wine. Thank you.

Thanks must also be given to Amy Bonnaffons, vastly overqualified proofreader (go read her amazing books, folks!) who helped me see through the messy forest of notes. Sarah Grossman at Cornell—thank you for taking on this project. J.C.—your illustrations are amazing. Thank you!

I would be remiss not to mention my old cat—Kattungen—whose steady snores kept me company while writing the last version of this book, and who then disappeared into the forest.

I am forever grateful to my mum, in whose old bedroom I write. Her no-nonsense feminist spirit and radical humanity is still felt by all who met her.

Of course, I also want to thank Kieve Saling, who moved halfway around the world with me, and then back again, never once doubting my ability (although at times, probably my sense of self-preservation).

Finally, and most importantly, I am forever indebted to the women and men interviewed, the ones facilitating the research, acting as translators, introducing me to people, generously sharing stories and experiences over countless cups of tea. This research could not have happened without them.

An earlier version of chapter 4 appeared in the journal *Citizenship Studies*.

Introduction

> **All Kachin people, we have freedom in our blood.**
> **Even if you kill us, kill our troops, you cannot take**
> **away our longing for freedom.**
>
> —Women's rights activist, Chiang Mai, 2016

The war in Kachinland is one of the longest-running wars in the world. It is an example of what scholars call an *intractable conflict*, a war that has been ongoing through generations and seems almost immune to resolution. From the outbreak of fighting in the early 1960s through today, hundreds of thousands of people have been displaced, and countless lives have been lost either through direct attacks or as a consequence of living through recurring cycles of war. Although the Kachin Independence Army (KIA), the armed wing of the Kachin Independence Organisation (KIO), has been called "one of the largest and most formidable of the ethnic armed groups" (International Crisis Group 2013), it should still be no match for the Myanmar state's military might, one of the largest armed forces in Southeast Asia, with an oversized budget and fervent support from the government. The KIO/KIA, however, have never been conquered. Indeed, one of the most puzzling aspects of the ongoing Kachin war lies in its very persistence.

This is all the more baffling given that mobilization and maintenance costs for armed political organizations remain high (Collier and Sambanis 2005; Wennmann 2011), especially when these organizations have to finance ongoing military deployment to defend themselves against state attacks *while* providing aid to those in displacement, as is the case with the KIO/KIA. As Paul Collier and Anke Hoeffler (2002) put it: "Potentially, finance is the only binding constraint on rebellion." Wars require, at a minimum, soldiers, vehicles, and weapons. Each soldier must be dressed, fed, and nursed. They need a home to defend and one to return to. They need phone money to call home and gas money for their motorbikes. They need shoes on their feet and families to dream of. They need children to be their future.

Given the magnitude of these needs, it is doubtful that the Kachin armed forces could rival the strength of the Myanmar military—by most accounts, one of the most well-resourced state militaries in the region. Yet somehow the KIO/KIA continue to mount a formidable resistance, year after year. How is this possible?

In the northern Thai town of Chiang Mai, which has long been a hub and a home for exiled Kachin activists and migrants, I began to piece together an answer. In the midst of teaching an English lesson to young students from Laiza and Mai Ja Yang who are interning with the Kachin Women's Association Thailand (KWAT), a women's rights organization, I ask them what women's duties are in the war that has once again resumed. One young woman puts her hand up and says, "Everything." "Everything?" I ask. "Like what?" The woman quickly reels off a long list of tasks, with other students filling in more answers: "They have to look after the children, they organize [prayer] groups for the soldiers at the frontline and they fast." "They have to make the uniforms and also in some areas do the cooking for the frontlines." "Women also mostly work in the IDP [internally displaced persons'] camps."

Someone else adds: "And they do all the social work too." "Women provide the love and the care and the passion and the moral support for men." "This," the young woman explains, "is the responsibility of women and very important right now." Yet, "this"—the everyday household labor and conduct of women living in the territory controlled by the Kachin armed forces—remains one of the least-understood parts of the conflict.

Scholars in feminist political economy have provided powerful and rich accounts of how women's reproductive labor matters to governance and state economies (Bedford and Rai 2010; Bhattacharya 2017; Federici 2012). When read alongside feminist work in Burma studies (Ikeya 2011; Tharaphi Than 2014, 2024) and research attending to everyday life under conditions of dictatorship and violence (Al-Khalili 2023; Ardeth Maung Thawnghmung 2019; Fink 2001; Nordstrom 1997), a picture emerges of women's labor as central to household and community survival in the midst of war. This focus helps us see how women, far from being submissive subjects, engage in actions and reactions to external structural changes, influencing not just their own lives but the lives of their communities as well (Ketola 2023; Mama and Okazawa-Rey 2012) in ways that are both profound and mundane, spectacular and intimate.

Across Southeast Asia, women have fought in independence movements, supported left-wing guerrilla struggles, and even led armed campaigns (Blackburn and Ting 2013; Lanzona and Rettig 2020; Parashar 2014), often combining traditional gendered roles with soldiering. Shirley Seng (2014), a founder of the KWAT, notes in her memoirs that after her marriage to one of the leaders of the KIA, she "had to cope with my baby and the revolutionary works [as best I could] . . . I made myself a revolutionary soldier and took the responsibilities I was assigned, since this was the Kachin National affair and revolution period." Yet women's participation has too often been read as being merely secondary or supportive, in effect obscuring both women and their labor from dominant stories about wars.

Understanding this labor, and the effect it has on everyday life as well as rebel objectives, is central to providing fuller and more accurate accounts of persistent rebel war, also beyond the Kachin borderlands. As Saw Mra Razar Lin (2019), fighting farther west on the Rakhine coast, recalls, "As a woman, it was not easy to try our best and we had to take on triple the burden of men. We had to give the time for our comrades while also giving time for social work and responsibilities for family and parents too."

As these exchanges so vividly illustrate, women's gendered social reproductive duties in the household, including cooking, child-rearing and "the care, the passion and moral support" they offer (as described by my students), play a significant role in sustaining not just individual soldiers but also the armed organization and the nation writ large. This suggests that reproductive work is not incidental to conflict but part of its very fabric. Kachin women's work within the setting of the ongoing war does not differ significantly from that of rural, revolutionary women elsewhere in Myanmar. Attention to the role gender plays in the conflict therefore offers a new perspective for understanding how the rebel wars, like the one in Kachinland, have been sustained and maintained for so long.

Reproducing the Revolution

My concept of *militarized social reproduction* augments current feminist research on social reproduction by extending the analysis to armed groups engaged in insurgency warfare. Importantly, different forms of militarized social reproduction inform and reinforce one another—to analytically distinguish between them does not mean that they are distinct in practice. Militarized social reproduction expands the concept of reproduction to include women's everyday labor undertaken in response to war, including military conscription, frontline provisioning, veteran care, and revolutionary marriage. I understand militarized social reproduction to be care work in displacement camps, where women often collectively work together to make ends meet, pooling their meager resources to provide for both immediate family members and soldiers far away on the battlefield. I understand it as daily labor on land lost in the war and in the conscription of daughters to the army on behalf of their brothers. I find it in the hundreds of marriages facilitated by the KIO to "engender loyalty and enthusiasm" (as many of my interlocutors put it) and in the encouragement to give birth for a community facing "genocidal attacks" (as the rebel leadership phrased it). This labor is not static but changes in relation to both the demands of the war and the life stages of the women involved in this labor: a young unmarried recruit might focus the bulk of her labor in the military where she is employed in a lower-ranking position as a nurse, seamstress, or a trainer, whereas a married wife living in displacement will spend most of her energy on a combination of housework, child-rearing, and money-making. Unlike other studies in the broad field of civil wars, rebel governance, or war studies, the application of militarized social reproduction renders visible how wartime gender orders are forged and (trans)formed through the labor and bodies of women and girls. This means that wars are shaped through everyday actions, and women's reproductive and productive labor help reproduce wartime orders, but not in a totalizing way: women can, and do, resist the demands of the Kachin leadership but also, importantly, the oppressive reach of Burmese state power.

The longer the conflict lasts, the more important women's reproductive activities become. The Kachin army, in at least some instances, can no longer afford to pay its soldiers on a regular basis—obligating the wives and daughters of male soldiers to engage in unsafe income-generating activities in order to send materials to soldiers on the front line. These income-generating activities often draw on the commercialization of women's social reproductive duties, resulting in women migrating abroad as maids, sex workers, and birth mothers, as recent reports have shown (Johns Hopkins Bloomberg School of Public Health and Kachin Women's Association Thailand 2018). This suggests that demands on women to sustain and resource the armed forces increase with the demands of the conflict, making this an even more urgent area of research. Yet, too often, a widespread focus on ethnicity, state-making, or the behavior of military elites have prevented observers and scholars from noticing the ways in which women's labor underpins the Kachin army's endurance.

The 2014 Myanmar Population and Housing Census indicates that a quarter to a third of all homes in government-controlled areas of Kachin State are female-headed (Myanmar Department of Population 2015a). Recent statistics from the United Nations indicate that about 80 percent of the population living in displacement in Kachin IDP camps are women and children (UN Office for the Coordination of Humanitarian Affairs 2016, 2017; UN Women 2021). In households that lack a male authority figure, men's absence is explained by drug addiction, conscription, or migration. In households that are de facto headed by women, men are present but unable to contribute to the household economy due to addiction, disease, or injuries. The women in these households are typically engaged in agriculture, informal trading, and casual labor.[1] Before their displacement to IDP camps, the majority of the women I interviewed in Kachinland worked in agriculture, undertook agriculture-related casual labor, or engaged in petty trading as their primary income source. In displacement, these women became reliant upon casual labor, remittances, and food aid.[2] The women in these households have had to shoulder a huge responsibility in ensuring the survival of their communities, suggesting that the Kachin household is an integral, if often overlooked, unit in the Kachin military project.

In Kachinland, the movement for equality and rights in the face of repeated attacks and disinvestment has come at an extraordinarily high cost. Kachin women and men I speak to say that no household has escaped the war, whether they live in proximity to it or not. The Kachin household is therefore a militarized and often dispersed household, where a sense of home and belonging is animated by women's labor, even as kinship relations are reframed by the war.

Kinship, constituted around the centrality of household and marriages, is reproduced through women's affective and material relations. It is traditionally understood "as a triangular system of families that can give brides (*mayu*), families that can take brides (*damau*), and families from whom brides can be neither given nor taken (*kahpu kanau*)" (Sadan 2024, 7). Yet repeated displacement and dispossession have changed household dynamics, as young people delay marriage, women manage households on their own, and military-organized mass weddings take on a new urgency. The realities of war irrevocably alter the possibilities and opportunities for life. As Sharika Thiranagama (2011, 12) succinctly puts it, writing about war and postwar Sri Lanka, "War grounds life even as it takes it away."

The concept of militarized social reproduction also helps us to see how these transformations in the war economy affect women, especially because direct deaths and casualties on the battlefields do not give a complete picture of what it means to live in and experience protracted war. The bodies of women tend to bear the long-lasting consequences of war, which affects their opportunities to reimagine and shape different political futures. The longevity of the war in northern Myanmar, alongside an absence of state welfare investments and infrastructural development, has taken a massive toll on the overall health and rights of people living in this conflict-affected borderland.

Women often shoulder the burden of making up for persistent gaps in resources; these gaps are severe and only grow wider as the insurgency goes on. Rebel groups like the Kachin army are not only responsible for their soldiers; they also have to provide for the civilians living in areas under their control.

This responsibility is compounded by the fact that in conflict-affected areas of northern Myanmar, almost one in seven people have had to flee attacks, unable to return back home. People living in displacement desperately need food, shelter, and health care. Yet aid is blocked by the Myanmar government from reaching camps controlled by the KIO where almost half of displaced people reside, most of them women and children.[3] Poverty, already dire, is increasing in the region, including in areas not directly affected by the fighting: the Integrated Household Living Condition Assessment (IHLCA) estimates that about 29 percent of the population in Kachin State lives below the poverty line (IHLCA 2011). The COVID-19 crisis has exacerbated vulnerabilities, as has the 2021 military coup, which led to an intensification of fighting in Kachin areas.

Whether women are soldiers themselves; wives, mothers, or daughters to soldiers; or simply civilians living in areas under the control of the Kachin armed forces, the tasks of care—often in addition to the tasks necessary to generate income—are often outsourced to them. The women I speak to in displacement camps are pooling their meager incomes to send to their sons and husbands on the front lines. They give birth in drafty shelters and sleep seven to a room under inadequate blankets. They cannot afford sanitary products, and they sling their children on their backs when they go to work, for meager pay, on the banana and sugarcane plantations dotting the countryside. They do backbreaking, seemingly never-ending work. They are paid less than men, if they are paid at all. A 2020 report notes that *if* displaced women in Kachin State find paid employment, their monthly income is 20 percent lower than displaced men and more than 30 percent lower than women not living in displacement (Durable Peace Programme Consortium 2020).

A young woman I met in Myitkyina illustrates the burden of militarized social reproduction on women and girls living in and through war. Her father was in the KIA, and her mother was a former soldier residing in a displacement camp with five of her children. In November 2015, the mother "took a Chinese pill" to induce an abortion when she realized she was pregnant again, as she felt unable to provide for yet another mouth. I met the young woman in March 2016; her mother was still bedridden. As the oldest child in the family, this young woman now had to assume all caretaking duties and had given up her dreams of attending university. She was thinking instead that despite the risks of trafficking, she should go to China to work as a maid, as the reduction in humanitarian aid meant that the needs of her family were not met despite her quitting school and trying to make an income through day labor.

Women are buckling under the strain to keep individual soldiers and the army writ large alive. This means that the longer the conflict drags on, the harder it becomes for women to (re)produce the revolution. Thus, understanding their work as contributors to militarization is important not only because it demonstrates broader and deeper linkages between a gendered political economy and the conduct of war but also because understanding this work as a form of militarized social reproduction brings into sharp relief the impact this labor has on the women themselves.

Reproducing Militarization through the Household

I use the term *household* throughout this book to refer to a dynamic, contested, gendered, and militarized space in which women's unpaid and undervalued duties sustain both the individual home and the armed revolution. This understanding is meant to illustrate how the household and its members, whether geographically close or far apart, support armed conflict through direct or indirect military work. Inspired by the work of international relations scholar Patricia Owens (2015), I conceptualize the conflict-affected household as a gendered, hierarchal, and dynamic entity and as an object of military strategy. Focusing on the political economy of the household means shining a spotlight on the gendered divisions of labor, power, resources, and identities produced and reproduced within it. Such a focus implies that the household is embedded within a political-economy context and is also a space for resistance and contestation. To paraphrase Owens (2015), household governance is always marked by resistance. In other words, households take a variety of forms and are not fixed, passive sites; they develop within and in response to changes both external and internal to the household—such as warfare, level of development, and types of welfare systems (Douglass 2012; Elias and Gunawardana 2013). The relationship between the household and the military is dynamic, uneven, and heterogenous, and at times troubled by women who resist gendered expectations of duty, care, and compliance with overarching military goals and objectives.

Moreover, women move among various types of households throughout their life course. For example, a women's rights activist in her early thirties I interviewed in 2015 detailed growing up without a father in the 1980s, as he was fighting for the KIO/KIA, leaving her mother to shoulder the responsibility for the survival of her family. During this time, the mother was engaged in a variety of informal activities to provide for her family, including opium and jade trading and subsistence agriculture. Once the ceasefire was agreed on in 1994, her father returned and the family moved to a government-controlled area where they earned stable revenue through white-collar work.

The impact of conscription and migration, as illustrated here, suggests that households are not geographically bounded but connected through affective and material relations (Howell 2015). This household remained a household even though its members were scattered.

Through various subsistence and reproductive activities, the mother in this family helped underpin the war effort by keeping the members of the household fed, dressed, and loved—whether they physically resided within the same space or not. This suggests two things: one, that kinship relations are critical for maintaining both households and broader communities across geographical differences, and, two, that these dynamics are transformed through war. Similar points also have been raised by other scholars of Myanmar borderlands and insurgent state-building, and I remain indebted to their work and insights (Dillabough-Lefebvre 2025; Ferguson 2021; Haokip 2023; Ong 2023; Rajah 2008; Sadan 2013a; Steinmüller 2022). Where I differ is in my feminist analysis of the household and its relationship to the political economy of war.

This means that I understand Kachin households as embedded in a military context that pushes the household to direct its activities toward servicing and sustaining the armed revolution and the imagined Kachin nation. Although this overarching political economy context is neither constant nor fixed, the war constitutes a key factor framing household behavior and responses. In other words, women's household duties, which feminist work on the household has demonstrated are essential for the effective running of the market, also form an integral part of militarization processes. Women's labor may be perceived as peripheral, but as we will see in this book, women (as daughters, mothers, and wives to soldiers, as well as being soldiers themselves) are central to the work of war.

Asking Feminist Questions about the War

Focusing on Kachin women as holders of knowledge means that I have been able to delve deep into questions concerning the gendered materiality of war. By asking questions about women's social reproductive and productive labor—what I in this book call *militarized social reproduction*—I have gained new insights into the meaning and making of war and have reimagined "the home front" as a space for the political, both in terms of enabling revolutions forward and sustaining everyday life. Alongside other feminist thinkers (Baines 2016; Enloe 2010; Nordstrom 1997), this has led me to the conclusion that we cannot understand wars unless we understand the lived experiences of wars—and, in particular, the ways in which women and girls in households supposedly disconnected from the front line are in fact embedded within and affected by military relations. In other words, the results gained from learning from women in Kachinland have far-reaching implications for how we understand and theorize civil wars.

This focus challenges the dominant narrative on Myanmar by researchers whose principal concern has been to listen to male voices, male soldiers, and male political leaders. Problematically, the emphasis on armies and on (male) soldiers hides the expansive and extensive work done by women in underpinning armed conflict. We know from research undertaken on women in armed movements across Southeast Asia that women participate in and experience wars in ways that "are consistently different from men," as Barbara Watson Andaya (2020, 268) puts it. Therefore, the primary research conducted with Kachin women for this book enables a novel analysis of how the war in Kachinland is understood and constructed by people otherwise marginalized in state-centric or androcentric accounts of civil wars in Myanmar.

Furthermore, the impact of unequal gendered responsibilities during wartime and the insecurities they give rise to are not unique to Kachin women but can be applied more broadly. Indeed, extant research on women in/around militaries around the world has noted how women's inclusion in military organizations tends to occur in such a way that the masculine boundaries and the masculinized dynamics of these units are not upset. These bodies of work show how, regardless of the extent of involvement of women in state or rebel organizations, pervasive gendered norms and dynamics mean that women are still typically subordinate to men, leading to discrimination, insecurity, and inequality (Enloe 2000; Yuval-Davis 1985). As Swati Parashar (2009) notes, "Armed militancy, therefore, is an opportunity for a few women to have a public presence, and yet it is an opportunity that seems to reinstate them further into the realm of the private." Narratives that celebrate or exceptionalize the agency of women who supposedly break gender boundaries through their participation in militancy, along with efforts that center women in military organizations, obfuscate the gendered dynamics of violence and exclusion that often are fundamental to the operations and legitimacy of militaries (Berry and Lake 2021, 472). Rather than upsetting gender hierarchies, women's participation might instead legitimatize military might and the patriarchal relations at their core.

Moreover, centering military institutions and soldiers in our analyses of war means that the way we study war might hide the extensive work and harm done outside the immediate vicinity of the battlefront. In long-term wars like those fought in Kachinland, unfolding across generations and households, war is experienced both as an everyday insecurity and in waves of direct attacks, as women like Seng Rai (her story is mentioned in the preface) struggle to keep their children and kin fed, clothed and safe, and with a future worth living for. Traditional approaches to the study of war—focusing on battlefield deaths and direct mortality, troop strengths and tactics, peace agreements and generals—are ill-equipped to deal with the presence of this violence in daily life (Sjoberg 2014), treating it as an exception or a singular event (Baines 2016). Also ill-equipped to account for the continuum of violence permeating war zones is an emphasis on sexual violence in conflict, often reported in the conflicts in Myanmar. A singular focus on wartime sexual violence sets it apart from other forms of violence, rendering it exclusive or spectacular while hiding or naturalizing other forms of violence (Eriksson-Baaz and Stern 2013), including more mundane, longer-term, and gendered effects of armed conflict. Such an approach also risks contributing "to a hierarchy of 'worthy' oppression, wherein some forms of harm and violence are more deserving of attention and outrage whereas others are not" (Berry and Lake 2021, 472).

In Kachinland, violence is present in the high rate of maternal mortality and the nutritional deficit of children born too early to mothers working too hard on sugarcane and banana plantations. It is present in unsafe migration patterns, in the thousands of young girls moving across the border to China as maids, wives, or surrogate mothers (Johns Hopkins Bloomberg School of Public Health and Kachin Women's Association Thailand, 2018). It is present in "exceptional" acts of sexual violence, shelling, and torture, but also the almost constant worry and fear for one's kin and loved ones. As Seng Rai's story illustrates, experiences of war cannot be reduced to singular or spectacular events but need to be understood as mundane experiences of violence threaded into and shaping daily life across generations.

In developing a feminist political-economy analysis of the Kachin conflict through the everyday experiences of women such as Seng Rai, this book provides both a theoretical and empirical contribution to studies of war and conflict. Taking the household seriously as a material relation and treating women as sources of knowledge engender a fresh approach to the gender dimensions of conflict and insecurity and may help explain just how wars, like those fought in Kachinland, have lasted for so long and with what effects.

Historical Context

> I was very young when the fighting between the KIA and the Burmese Army started, but we soon all felt the effects of it. . . .
> It was not unknown for people to be shot on their doorsteps at this time. We felt that the Burmese were invaders occupying our land.
> — Nhkum Bu Lu (2016, 293)

One evening after fieldwork, sitting around a fire, I asked one of my friends what "Mung maden, gumsheng, Myen Asuya" translated as. I knew the phrase referred to the Myanmar government and had heard it used plenty, but since I could not speak Jinghpaw, I was not sure how it translated *exactly*. My friend thought for a while and then explained that it translated as "the Colonial/Invader Ruthless/ Aggressive Dictator Burmese Government."

Ah, I thought to myself, that makes sense. This phrase captures the fractured relations that have been at the heart of Kachinland's relationship to Myanmar since independence.

Kachinland, or Wunpawng Mungdan, is located in the green hills of north-ernmost Myanmar. Unlike Kachin State, which borders neighboring Shan State to the east, China to the north, and India to the west, Kachinland ignores these official national and international borders and stretches much farther. Although both Kachin State and Kachinland are sparsely populated, with most people liv-ing in rural communities, the Kachin population is nevertheless one of the most politically important minority groups in Myanmar today. Kachinland has never been fully incorporated into Myanmar proper but has, over six decades of war, retained relative autonomy (Sadan and Maran 2022).

The idea of Wunpawng Mungdan has been deployed (at times, forcefully so) as the imagined nation for which one fights, rationalizing the use of both arms and claims to political rights. As with Shanland (Ferguson 2021) or Kawt-hoolei (Garbagni and Walton 2020; Rajah 2002; South 2007) farther south[4]— where ethnonationalist struggles emerged sometime after independence from the British—Wunpawng Mungdan has been understood as an elite attempt to construe pan-Kachin identity at the expense of other minority identities and languages present in the area (Sadan 2013) where wars have been fought, on and off, for decades.

As Nhkum Bu Lu recalls above, the wars in this region—the northernmost area of Myanmar—have a long history of invasion and occupation. The war in Kachinland began in 1961 after the Burman-dominated leadership in central Myanmar made attempts to outlaw minority languages and practices. This was the final straw for ethnic populations, such as the Kachin, who felt betrayed by the government's failure to deliver on promises made in negotiations for inde-pendence from the British in 1948. In the lead-up to the negotiations, Kachin politicians had debated how and in what ways Kachin independence would best be ensured, finally agreeing that participation in the Panglong Agreement would bring about social and economic justice and elevate Kachin State to an equal partner in the Union of Burma (Sadan 2013).[5] These promises were not delivered, and by the time of the 1960 elections, there was a widespread sense of disappoint-ment among not only Kachin communities but also ethnic minorities across the country with the new political order (Ralph and Sheera 2019; Sadan 2013). More and more ethnic minority leaders called for renewed political dialogues or armed

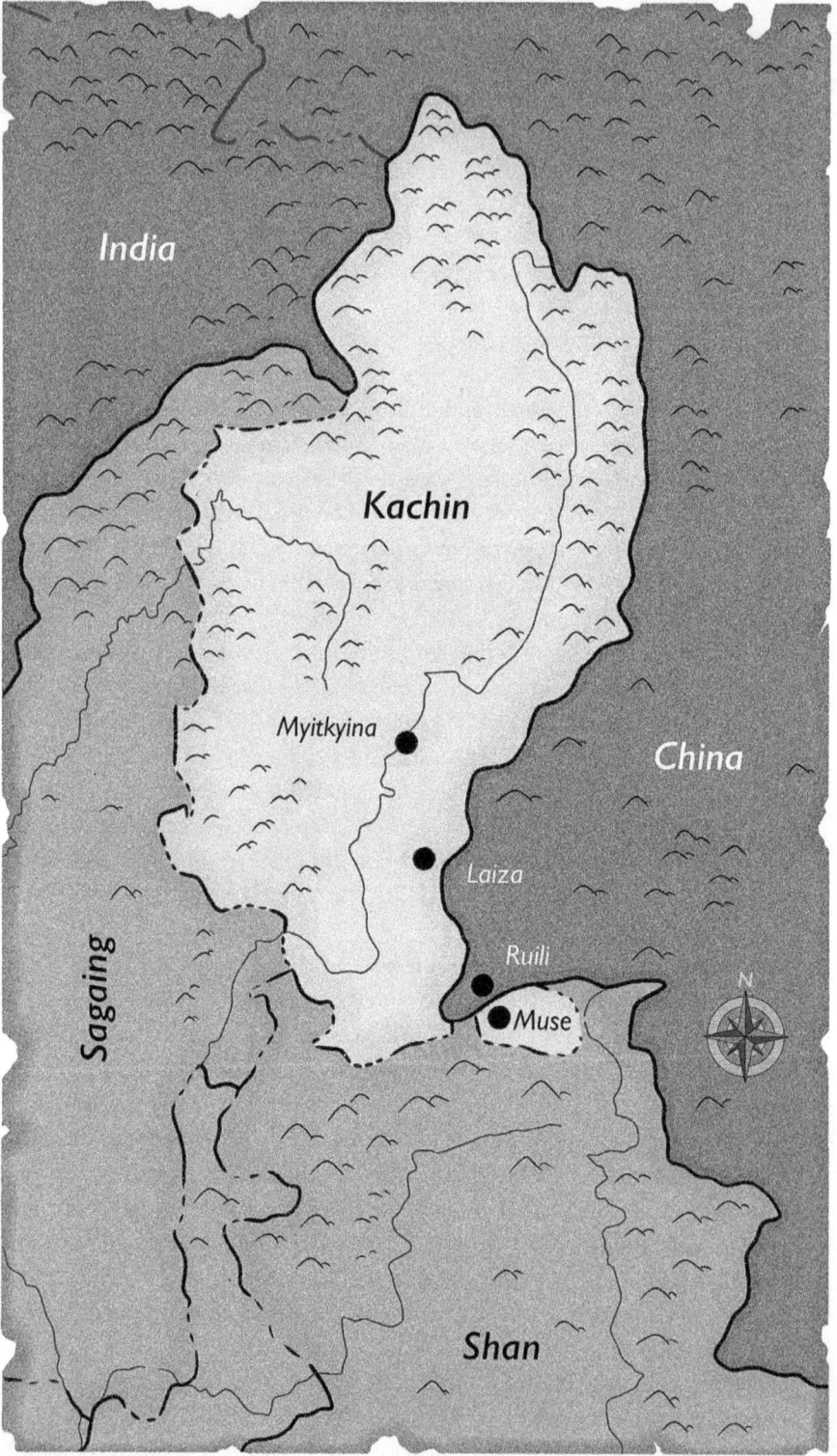

FIGURE 1. Map of Kachinland.

uprisings. This greatly alarmed the head of the Burmese military, General Ne Win, who in 1962 took power in a coup (Smith 1999).

Members of an underground movement of Kachin university students called the Seven Stars had already begun talking of an armed uprising, and in February 1961, a select few met in Lashio to formally and openly declare an armed revolution. The few attendees agreed on the following objectives, as recounted in Major N'Chyaw Tang's unpublished memoir:

1. To establish the republic of Kachinland,
2. To drive out the invader Burman imperialists from the Kachinland, and
3. To make viable the armed Kachin independence army perfectly, thus this very day has become the KIA day or the resistance day.

A month later, as recalled by Major N'Chyaw Tang, the Seven Stars raided the Lashio treasury, raising enough funds to set up the first military training camp with seventy-two new male recruits. As recounted in the major's memoirs, many missions followed: to China and India as well as to other ethnic communities to raise funds, access weapons, build alliances, and unite a disparate Kachin community under the Kachin cause. Social practices were reinterpreted, as the old system of hereditary chiefs (*duwas*) was replaced by a "uniformed military leadership" (Maran La Raw 2007, 43). As will be discussed more in chapter 4, attempts were also made to lower or ban the dowry and encourage marriages across the ethnic subgroups included under the Kachin umbrella. Alongside the invention of a "monumental Kachin flag"[6] and other national symbols and rituals, these practices constituted attempts by the new Kachin leadership to foster unity around a Kachin armed cause (Sadan 2013, 336–37).

In the following years, the Seven Stars grew from a loosely organized network of students and civilians-with-arms into one of Myanmar's largest armed organizations, the KIA. A political wing, the KIO, was established to maintain a de facto government in liberated areas of northern Myanmar with departments of education, justice, health, and so on, areas that are under the control of the KIO/KIA. As we will look at in more detail in the following chapters, recruits were drawn from the household, with each family expected to contribute a son or a daughter to the cause, and a "war tax" was set up to help fund the Kachin military apparatus. As repeated displacement, injury, and military service led to changes in household dynamics, kinship relations were further reimagined. In the absence of husbands, women became heads of households; young soldiers, finding dowries to be prohibitively costly, cohabited outside of marriage; and military officers (*du ni*) stepped in to negotiate marriage proposals (Maran La Raw 2007). A Jinghpaw-defined model of kinship took on increasing importance (Sadan 2013). The war thus generated new ways of being, as social norms and codes related to marriage and household relations were reproduced and reinterpreted in relation to broader changes and disruptions to everyday life.

As in all civil wars, civilians suffered the brunt of these conflicts. Tens of thousands of people were displaced. Parts of Kachin State were declared free-fire zones by the junta, with state troops sanctioned to shoot any civilian on sight. Whole villages were burned down. A Human Rights Watch report (1992) notes extensive abuses committed by the state military, such as summary executions, torture, portering, sexual violence, and forced relocation of Kachin civilians to military-controlled villages. State policies aimed at eradicating resistance also included nonmilitary means of subjugation, including targeting places of minority religious practice, disallowing the teaching of ethnic languages, and arresting anyone assumed to have rebel connections. A mother of six, currently living in a displacement camp in the north of the country, recalled when, at the age of ten, her village was torched by the Burmese military. She explained that after the burning of her village, "We were forced to move to a military camp, but without my father who had been tortured by the military." She never saw her father again.

In short, the impact of the war on everyday life was as devastating as it was monumental. A woman I spoke to in 2016 summarized those years simply: "We ran—all the time." Later, she retold a story her mother had shared with her about how she was usually a "good baby," but "whenever we had to pass the Burma Army posts I cried! She would have to cover my mouth with her hand, and one time almost killed me by accident because she covered my mouth for too long." A member of the Seven Stars, an elderly gentleman with dyed jet-black hair and a slight tremor in his voice, told me when we sat in his kitchen in late 2015 that during this period "they will arrest every [Kachin] man they see in the street, this is the Burmese way." Other, younger people I spoke to remembered growing up hiding in bunkers and fields.

In 1994, a ceasefire between the central government and the KIO/KIA was agreed upon. The reasons leading up to this have been well documented; they include wider geopolitical events such as the disintegration of the communist bloc and changes in relations with Thailand and China, as well as a general war-weariness on both sides. The many decades of armed conflict had devastated areas under KIO control. As the historian Mandy Sadan (2016) notes, KIA soldiers, often stationed in rural areas, had become "increasingly isolated" from the very populations they set out to fight for, especially those residing in urban communities. However, while the ceasefire did lead to a reduction in direct conflict, which made everyday life easier, especially for those residing in rural communities who now could travel more freely and did not have to worry as much about forced recruitment by the KIO/KIA, it did not resolve any underlying political issues, and many people I spoke to continued to experience land insecurity, poverty, inequality, and discrimination.[7] This led some commentators to refer to the ceasefire period commencing in 1994 as a period of "armed peace" (Sadan 2016). Extensive underdevelopment, pervasive land grabbing, and increases in drug addiction and communicable diseases contributed to feelings of dissatisfaction and frustration associated with the outcome of the ceasefire. A young female captain I met in 2013 simply shrugged her shoulders when I asked her about the ceasefire years: "Ahh, that was nonsense."

While the 1994–2011 ceasefire did not resolve larger political issues, or indeed bring peace to everyday lives, it provided a space for Kachin society to respond to community needs. This period saw the emergence of new forms of civilian opposition and a resurgence of organized civil society and youth activism with ties to the KIO/KIA. As will be discussed in chapter 4, this proved important when the conflict resumed in 2011, as the KIO/KIA could capitalize on burgeoning nationalistic sentiments among youth (Jones 2016; Sadan 2015; Smith 2016). Meanwhile, the military junta began to engage in a number of state-building exercises. These included the launch of their "roadmap to democracy," which purported to lay out how the country would transition from an outright dictatorship to a military-controlled form of government, using the trappings of democratic governance. The KIO had attended the National Convention leading up to the writing of a new constitution, proposing a return to the principles of the Panglong Agreement, including the right of internal self-determination and the fundamental rights of all ethnic nationalities (EBO 2010). This was ignored, and in 2008, the military junta put forward a new constitution, ensuring a controlled transition toward an authoritarian mode of "disciplined democracy" where 25 percent of the new legislature would be occupied by military men. The new constitution required all armed groups to surrender their arms and come under the control of the Burmese army as so-called Border Guard Forces or People's Militia Forces (Buchanan 2019; Ardeth Maung Thawnghmung 2011). The KIO/KIA, along with several other armed groups, resisted this and began to repopulate their ranks with new young soldiers. The KIO also drew up a number of counterproposals, submitted to the military junta, stating that it was willing to become a member of a "Union Defence Force" if the spirit of the Panglong Agreement were upheld and the rights and self-determination of ethnic minorities respected. Once again, its proposals were rejected (EBO 2010). Tensions between the KIO/KIA and the Myanmar military increased.

In 2010, popular elections were held to usher in the new military-controlled government, which took its seat in 2011. The move from an outright dictatorship also included political and economic reforms as well as a peace process initiated in 2011 (Thant Myint-U 2019). However, also in 2011, the Burmese military attacked Kachin army outposts after the deadline for the KIO to transform into a Border Guard Force passed (Sadan 2016). This effectively ended the ceasefire that had lasted almost two decades. War again ensued, with the KIO/KIA benefiting from the resurgence of nationalistic support among predominantly young people to fight the state. As one of the women I interviewed put it: "You can demolish KIO [and] KIA, but if you can't give equality, and the rights that ethnic people demand, then a new KIO, a new KIA will be come up tomorrow."

As I am writing this, in 2024, the violence in Kachinland has taken a new turn. In February 2021, the Myanmar military resumed power in a coup. The subsequent impact on civilian communities has been particularly stark. Nearly 10 percent of the population in Kachin State are displaced. As noted earlier, 80 percent of those currently living in displacement camps are women and children.[8] Since April 2016, the government has restricted humanitarian aid from reaching IDP camps in KIO-controlled territory, increasing the strain on women heads of households to provide for their families in war-affected areas.[9] Poverty is widespread and worsening. The mother of six, cited above, said to me: "I have dealt with fighting and war all my life, since the coup my life has become even more difficult." She continued: "In 2011, I thought my life had become somewhat stable, but once the war resumed, I had to flee again. The only difference in my life now and before the coup, is that before the coup we had more humanitarian aid [in the displacement camp], and now we don't have any." Clashes are also escalating, including air strikes against Kachin civilians, like the attack in October 2022 on an outdoor concert celebrating the founding of the KIO. More than one hundred people died in what became known as the A Nang Pa massacre.

In the aftermath of the attack, a close friend explained, through tears, that "all life we have to deal with this, this injustice and this violence. It never, ever ends." After a pause, she said: "I always advocate for peace, but when you are from a minority group, and you are being attacked, how do you survive without an armed defense? In order to resist and survive, in order to make these broader changes, you have to first survive." She went on to quote the Indian scholar Gayatri Chakravorty Spivak, who wrote: "Sometimes situations become so intolerable that moral certainties are no longer meaningful" (Evans and Spivak 2016).

The protracted and severe nature of the war is playing a significant role not just in everyday lives but also in national-level politics, where the central government seems unable or unwilling to yield to rebel demands for equality and recognition, yet cannot defeat them either. The prospect of peace seems to be a long way off.

Feminist Research on War

Like all studies of war and revolutions, mine is an incomplete account, shaped by my biases, relationships, and emotions. As a PhD student venturing out on fieldwork in 2015, I wanted to understand how women's intimate knowledge and everyday experiences of war could help broaden understandings of war—how they begin; why they last; and, therefore, how they might end. The Kachin war seemed to provide an opportunity to do this. But I first came to this question not as a PhD student but as a volunteer on the Thai-Myanmar border.

In the mid-2000s, I was based for several years in northern Thailand, volunteering for women's organizations, including the KWAT. In fact, it was discussions with members of the KWAT and other Burmese women's organizations that first made me interested in learning more about the experiences of women in the armed forces in Myanmar. Several of the women I worked with were members of both women's rights organizations and armed groups, and between them had decades of experience of soldiering. Yet at the time of my work in Thailand, I did not see their histories reflected in accounts of Myanmar's many civil wars and revolutions, which, by and large, tended to assume that soldiering and resistance are male experiences. Luckily, this has changed in the years since, and I am indebted to feminist scholars and activists exploring the "herstories" of upheavals, nationalism, and war in Myanmar (Harriden 2012; Ikeya 2011; Tharaphi Than 2014).

Taking a cue from Sara Ahmed, who proposes that citation serves as feminist memory, I largely draw on feminist work to analyze my research findings. Ahmed (2017, 15–16) writes that "citation is how we acknowledge our debt to those that came before; those who helped us find our way. . . . Citations can be feminist bricks: they are the materials through which, from which, we create our dwellings." As a consequence, the vast majority of works cited in this book are written by feminist scholars who are, for the most part, women.

As this book builds on and adds to feminist studies in international relations, war studies, and political economy, it is grounded in a feminist tradition of taking the knowledge of women seriously. Considering the lack of Kachin women in both formal and informal governance settings in Myanmar, as well as the dearth of historical accounts recording the experiences of minority women living in conflict areas in Kachinland, valuing Kachin women as sources of knowledge has been crucial in order to capture, as Annick Wibben (2011, 100) puts it, "varied meanings of security as experienced in everyday circumstances." In other words, interviewing and observing Kachin women helps to highlight an otherwise forgotten dimension of the conflict. This book is concerned with bringing to the fore the lifeworlds of women living through war, centering them as complex holders of knowledge and experience that can inform more nuanced and ethical understandings of wars and their effects. This approach was also informed by the feminist conviction that for women to be involved in peace and political settlements, they need to be acknowledged as actors and participants in the conflict, their experiences recorded and included. Knowledge is, after all, the basis for action (DeVault and Gross 2012; Harding 1992).

As a result, I spent a lot of time learning from women on the ground. While the overarching questions guiding this research concern the role the Kachin household—and, in particular, women's household labor—plays in sustaining the war effort, multiple other questions emerged during the course of the research. These include: How does women's labor sustain the "normal" functions of Kachin society (that must go on despite the ongoing presence of conflict and without a government safety net)? Why and how do women's household duties inform or limit their participation in armed conflict? What roles have women's groups played in sustaining Kachin society? How have these groups enabled and/or circumscribed women's active participation in society? How do marriage practices affect women's ability to contribute labor to the war effort? What is the effect of women's labor on their bodies and mental health?

This multiplicity of questions came about as I learned more about the gendered roles and experiences of women in their everyday lives. The relationship between gendered roles and the changes in the conflict is in fact no accident, as I will show in the following chapters; gender roles have shifted and changed in relation to the broader objectives of the war efforts. I do not seek to provide explanations that hold true for all households or all women living in Kachinland; rather, I use this range of questions to generate a context from which I can sketch out a possible answer as to how and why the Kachin conflict has been sustained for so long, across life courses, generations, and households, and in the face of extensive and brutal state violence. As Juanita Elias and Shirin Rai (2015, 426) remind us: "It is the lived experiences of those on the ground that generate the most useful insights that enable us to connect everyday acts and forms of violence to broader political-economic structures and systems." This includes, in my reading, the political-economy apparatus of armed groups. Thus, through this focus on women's lived experiences, I am able to highlight the gendered role of women (whether as soldiers themselves, or as mothers, wives, and daughters to soldiers) as relevant actors and the household as a critical if overlooked site for conflict sustenance in studies of Myanmar, war, and security.

Writing (Revolutionary) Women's Worlds

The data for this book is drawn from semistructured interviews and participant observation collected during several trips to both Thailand and Myanmar. The first two of these trips were undertaken in 2013 and 2014, and I interviewed (mostly) female soldiers in the KIO/KIA about their experiences and perspectives on armed duty, war, and peace-building. These sets of interviews made me curious to further explore the role of women in the Kachin armed conflict, which I set out to do in my doctoral studies commencing in 2015. For my doctoral research, I returned to KIO-controlled areas in 2015 and 2016, and then again in 2017 and 2018, to dwell deeper on questions of gender and war. Speaking to women living through repeated waves of violence made me realize just how central women's labor has been to survival in the midst and aftermath of war, leading me to explore the role the Kachin household, and women's household labor, play in sustaining war efforts across space and time. In 2019, 2021, and 2023, I undertook further interviews remotely, with the invaluable aid of a local research assistant to probe around questions of marriage and marriage practices and to ask about life in displacement after the coup. In addition to these interviews, undertaken primarily with female soldiers and women living in displacement camps, I interviewed women and men active in different types of administrative roles within the KIO, advisers to members of the KIO Central Committee, students attending schools run by the KIO's educational department, local Kachin research organizations, and leaders and rank-and-file soldiers of other armed groups sharing territory with the KIO/KIA. I also spoke to members of local civil society, including Kachin women's organizations and had numerous informal (as well as formal, recorded) conversations with people working for different UN agencies and international nongovernmental organizations posted to Kachin State. I read and analyzed reports published by international agencies and local organizations; attended meetings and commemorations; taught at schools run by movement actors; and, as I have done sporadically since I left Chiang Mai in 2008, volunteered with women's groups.

These trips also included research undertaken in areas under Myanmar government control, such as Yangon and Myitkyina, and Chiang Mai and Bangkok in Thailand, where large populations from the Kachin community can be found. Here I interviewed members of the Kachin women's movements, the KIO foreign affairs department, as well as nongovernmental organizations and networks working in Kachin State, such as the Nyein Foundation, the Alliance for Gender Inclusion in the Peace Process, and the Kachin State Women's Network. In total, I interviewed more than one hundred women (and some men), using either English or Jinghpaw and Burmese. Of course, this research also resulted in certain blind spots—most, if not all, of my friends and colleagues are Christian, speak Jinghpaw, and identify as Kachin. However, the Kachin nation is made up of people from different subgroups who speak different languages; indeed, the exonym *Kachin* is highly contested and politicized. And as Mandy Sadan and Ja Htoi Pan Maran (2022, 326) note: "The boundaries, nomenclature, and degree of incorporation of . . . groups within the Kachin umbrella have shifted and continue to shift over both time and space." Engaging with other groups would no doubt have broadened the analysis, yet my connection to Kachin Jinghpaw-speakers made it challenging to meet individuals who would not self-identify as Kachin, not least because I did not have any prior relationships with them. The influence of religion is another important issue I did not delve deeply into, yet given the important role afforded the churches, feminist work undertaken within Kachin theological colleges and religious associations is critical for future research exploring gender issues in Kachinland. As this book concerns the gendered household and its (dynamic and, at times, conflictual) relationship with the military organization, the KIO/KIA, a more focused study of language and kinship relations would have been fruitful. Future research will hopefully delve more deeply into feminist stories of militarized kinship[10] and the gendered effects of language policies.

An obvious limitation of this research is my inability to speak Jinghpaw or Burmese. When the interviews were not conducted in English, I worked with Kachin interpreters, most of them women and most of them known to me either from previous work and connections to the area or from the organization where they were based. Importantly, they were also well known and respected in their communities. These women would also help organize interviews undertaken in liberated areas where it was difficult for me as a foreigner to move around on my own. In areas controlled by the Thai government or the Myanmar State, I typically set up my own interviews through previous connections with the Kachin women's movement or Kachin or ethnic minority political leaders. When interviews had been conducted in a language other than English, I would cross-check the translation with an external interpreter I knew from the KWAT, sending her anonymized audio files to transcribe or checking in with her about specific terms or words used. However, I did not only rely on the answers in the interviews; I also paid attention to broader power relations present in the community. I was able to observe the heavy labor undertaken by women inside and near the displacement camps, and I noted the absence of men. I observed young students building bunkers and getting dressed up for commemorative days and noticed how female soldiers interacted in the military when I visited. This allowed me to discern and trace the effects of a gendered division of labor on both women and the military writ large.

Without the prior connections and history with members of the Kachin resistance movements, as well as with other organizations based in the territory controlled by the Kachin army, such as the All Burma Students' Democratic Front, I would not have been able to do the kind of careful empirical research I set out to do in liberated areas, aiming to capture the everyday lived experiences of women. These areas are officially out of bounds for foreign researchers, and my relationships with movement actors, including armed organizations, were instrumental in facilitating access. This shared history also helped me fill in the gaps and parse the details of what I saw and learned with what I already knew of the gender dynamics in these movements, and it alleviated some of the issues associated with being a researcher not from the community.

Clearly, I am an outsider, not affected by the issues and insecurities many of the women I spoke to experience in their everyday lives. Being honest (with myself) about the limitations this outside position imposes on my research—in particular, my inability to fully grasp what it means to live through persistent war—I never imagined myself fully knowledgeable and was aware of the gaps in my research and understanding. At the same time, being an outsider was not always a detriment to the research; at times, it was beneficial. Not being from the community helped draw my attention to everyday practices and processes that an insider might not notice (Chua 2019). For example, one time early on in my research, I was asking after the gendered division of labor in and around the armed forces, and I was told that men and women contributed equally to the military cause. During a break in the interview, I wandered into a building adjacent to the office where I was met by rows of women at sewing machines, making uniforms. For me, this emphasized both the feminized support role that militarized women engage in and the invisibility of women's labor; for the women I interviewed, this was simply the status quo and not worth mentioning. At other times, young women would confide in me about their dissatisfaction with the KIO, levying critiques against the leadership or sharing experiences of sexual assaults within the army—phenomena I am not sure would have been disclosed had I been an insider or—perhaps even more challenging—a Burmese researcher.

In this way, although the interviews provided the foundation for the research, they were not privileged as the only source of knowledge. Neither were they situated as absolute truth. As Lee Ann Fujii (2010, 234) argues: "The value of people's narration about their experiences of violence—what they saw, did, felt, or heard—does not necessarily lie in their 'accuracy' or 'truthfulness.'" The value lies in the subjective meaning and the overall context that makes that interpretation of events important. This is particularly true in contexts of violence and conflict when emotions like fear or anger or political agendas around the war shape what is being told, how it is being told, and why. For example, all but one of the female soldiers I spoke to told me they had voluntarily enlisted in the armed forces. When I asked follow-up questions about the details of the enlistment procedures, I realized that most of them were in fact drafted "on behalf of their families," and sometimes forcefully so. To me, this illustrated the need to tell a specific war story—one in which women (voluntarily!) signed up to fight the Burman military—and rendered visible how military duty is a form of gendered labor. Thus, this focus on the ways in which the interactions among gender, power, and conflict frame how people make sense of their experiences rather than on the veracity of specific stories added an important piece to the puzzle that is the war in Kachinland.

As my understanding grew, I began to feel a discomfort with how the categories of civilian/soldier were applied in research on the Kachin civil war, freezing and delineating singular identities that I had begun to conceive of as relational and dynamic: many women I met moved between these categories, first as soldiers themselves and later as civilian wives-to-soldiers but still supporting the revolution materially and emotionally. I was equally uncomfortable with the ways in which the insecurity experienced by the women I had spoken to was frequently reduced to a single, often spectacular event in reporting on the war (see Baines 2016, 5). On the contrary, for many of these women, the close-to-two decades of the armed ceasefire leading up to the resumption of conflict in 2011 were but a brief interlude in an otherwise violent history that stretched across generations (see Sadan 2016). Fixed conceptualizations, I came to realize, are problematic because they shortchange our knowledge of war and prevent us from seeing how it unfolds across life courses, generations, and households.

I also had to learn how to grapple with contradictions that emerged from my feminist sentiments as a Swedish antimilitarist researcher (see Hoang 2015, 192). For many of the women I met, participation in the armed revolution was understood as an act of duty and care toward one's kin and future generations. As a former (female) soldier put it: "I thank God for choosing me to be part of the revolution. It wasn't easy but even now, I am ready to serve if needed. I know this is important." With respect and recognition of Kachin women's work and the ways in which they made sense of their experiences, I moved beyond the narrow script of equality and feminist politics I had been raised within and toward one that took seriously the notion that for some people, participation in armed revolutions is congruent with care and, in some instances, with feminist politics. Taking inspiration from Saba Mahmood (2001), in this book, I try to "imagine the politics of gender equality when situated within particular life worlds, rather than speak from a position of knowledge that already knows what the undoing of inequality would entail." This means building knowledge from the ground up, allowing the "particular" to guide and make possible theorizations about wars and their gendered effects rather than leaning on our "academic vantage points" to explain social phenomena (Lal 1999, 107). I agree with Lee Ann Fujii (2009, 29), who writes in her study on the Rwanda genocide that "political scientists often underestimate the value of knowledge about the 'particular' or 'local,' assuming such findings to be too closely tied to specific times and places to be generalizable. This assumption is false." Indeed, it is precisely from the particular and the specific that we can generate new and complex theorizations about the world, tracing the relationship between contradictory and sometimes chaotic realities and the making and effects of war.

Focusing on women's lived experiences as a way to understand and approach the study of war engendered practical, methodological, and ethical dilemmas. As Elisabeth J. Wood (2006, 373) notes:

> The ethical imperative of research ("do no harm") is intensified in conflict zones by political polarization, the presence of armed actors, the precarious security of most residents, the general unpredictability of events, and the traumatization through violence of combatants and civilians alike.

Thus, the challenges of undertaking sensitive research cannot be alleviated simply by adherence to university or administrative ethics approvals (Pittaway, Bartolomei, and Hugman 2010; Fujii 2012) or what Guillemin and Gillam (2004) aptly refer to as "procedural ethics." Instead—not in its place but as an addition—I developed a contextual ethical framework, one in which consent and control over the interview situation was stressed, and the knowledge of the research participants over their local context was emphasized. Paying attention to positionality, power, and relationship, I verbally asked for and received informed consent ahead of, during, as well as after the interview, stressing to the respondents that they were ultimately in control of the interview, meaning that they could choose to terminate the interview altogether at any moment in time, and only answer questions if they felt comfortable doing so. I purposefully never asked for information about possibly traumatic events but kept questions broad, allowing the women I spoke with to decide the direction of the interview. I continuously

checked in and discussed issues of security and ethics with the people participating in my research, asking them how they understood in/security and what
I should do to avoid encountering or causing it, whether for them or for myself
(see Fujii 2012). In order to protect the people participating in this research project, I did not write down the names of anyone I met, and in this book all names
as well as the exact date and location of the interviews are withheld; synonyms or
simply a descriptor of the role held—officer, former soldier, student, and so on—
are instead used. I explained that their stories and experiences might feature in
academic publications, but also form a core part of advocacy and public outreach
about the situation in Kachinland, if they so wished. I told them to let me know
if they changed their mind about participation, that I would be happy to remove
their input from any future publications. No one ever contacted me about this.

Feminist Fieldwork Failures

Yet even with these preparations, I encountered several ethical dilemmas. In
my first round of interviews undertaken with female soldiers, I gained access
to participants through the approval of their higher-ups. These sets of interviews were conducted on military bases in liberated areas, and I was told they
had to be sanctioned by the head of the brigade, or else the women might
run the risk of reprisals. Trusting my interlocuters, I agreed, and while I duti-
fully informed the women who came to speak to me about the possibility of
withdrawing and emphasized the voluntary nature of their participation, they
were clearly not there voluntarily since the soldiers most likely had received
orders rather than requests. This highlighted the difficult position of trying
to make ethical choices during fieldwork: If I had not asked for approval from
higher-ranking members of the organization to undertake these interviews,
the women participating might have run the risk of disciplinary action; if
I asked for approval from higher-ranking members, the women's participation could not be seen as fully voluntary; if I did not do these interviews,
their stories would not be told (to me, at least). Unable to resolve this ethical
conundrum, on subsequent trips to Kachinland, I did very few interviews
with active female soldiers, focusing instead on former soldiers and military
members of the administration I would come across in settings outside army
bases. While I feel a degree of unease with my decision to avoid doing interviews on military bases, I agree with Jayati Lal (1999), who writes: "These contradictions constitute an essential component of the process of doing social
science research in the 'real' world."

There was another challenge related to emotional dynamics, which affected my research in multiple, sometimes confusing ways. Feelings of fear, uncertainty, guilt, and hopelessness framed some of the interviews I undertook as part of my PhD project. I found myself conflating research participants' needs with my own: my hopelessness about the war made me want to intervene in direct ways, as the vignette in the preface makes clear. I felt guilty for not helping; yet no one ever asked me to do anything other than to listen and observe. My confusion and my fear led me to cut some interviews short. Believing I was harming women who displayed crisis responses, I would turn off the recorder instead of asking them what they wanted to do. There was another transfer of emotions too: my thoughts about the conflict and my need to leave it mirrored their imaginings, their wishes to leave it all behind, to go home. Of course, they could not. I could, and I did. Centering emotions in my methodological approach helped me see their impact on both data collection and analysis while facilitating an examination of how the war was experienced, and responded to, in the everyday (Hedström 2018).

Another source of ethical confusion was how to act when confronted with statements that did not hold true for me. For example, during my first research trip to liberated areas, the woman I had initially planned to travel with to help set up interviews had to cancel at the last minute; instead, I was introduced to a man in his forties. It quickly became apparent that he did not think much of my research or, what he dismissed as, "Western feminist privileges." He was also a homophobe and made several derogatory slurs about Aung San Suu Kyi, a leading figure in the pro-democracy movement and, later, state counselor, playing on her gender. I did not say anything when he made those comments. I also did not say anything when he assumed I was a fellow Christian and asked me to give thanks for the food served. My prior methodological training had led me to stress empathy and trust as important in research, but here I had neither empathy (for his views) nor honesty (about my religious beliefs). Similar to the female soldiers mentioned above—who were actively creating an image of voluntary rather than forced participation in the armed forces—the incident with this man illustrates how the people we engage in our research are not simply responding to us but actively shaping what we learn as researchers, choosing to tell some "truths" while hiding others (Lal 1999). As Lee Ann Fujii (2009, 42) points out: "How people talk about the world—whether true or not—gives clues as to how they make sense of that world—how it is and how it ought to be."

Rather than resolving these "dilemmas," we need to approach our research process and the knowledge generated from it as constituting partial truths and conflicting subject positions that, taken together, can tell us something important and new about how social phenomena such as war are justified, experienced, and carried out. In this way, by being honest about the messiness and failures of doing research, we may move toward the creation of more complex knowledge that is able to account for the contradictory and chaotic world we live in.

Chapter Overview

In the chapters that follow, I explore how women support the revolution materially, symbolically, emotionally, and legally at different stages in their lives. This book begins with chapter 1 introducing one aspect of militarized social reproduction, *militarized care*, to help explain the processes by which Kachin women's labor maintains the Kachin military effort by women living in army brigades and in displacement. I discuss how women's care sustains the lives of communities both in liberated areas and internal displacement camps, and I trace ways that Kachin women work outside the household to generate income for the war effort. In chapter 2, I turn to the women's wing of the Kachin armed forces, the Kachin Women's Association (KWA), outlining the history of the organization and the role it has played in different cycles of the war. I explore how the military has drawn on the KWA to generate militarized social reproduction in support of rebel needs and discuss how the KWA both empowers and circumscribes women's participation in the broader war effort. Chapter 3 homes in on the experiences of women soldiers, and, using the concept of *militarized labor*, I examine the ways in which their roles within the military parallel and naturalize their domestic roles in the household. I find that while women's military participation waxes and wanes in relation to the broader demands of the war efforts, women's military mobilization consistently draws on and reasserts a gendered division of labor, which positions women as undervalued and/or unwaged workers largely responsible for the social reproduction of the household and the army. Chapter 4 asks what this gendered division of labor means for the cadres of young female soldiers who have joined the KIO/ KIA since the outbreak of war in 2011. Although female soldiers may face both stigma and suspicion, they navigate the insecurity they experience by becoming even more committed and loyal soldiers. Chapter 5 looks at what happens once women, upon marriage to soldiers, leave the KIO/KIA, demonstrating how *militarized marriage* forms another critical part of militarized social reproduction, helping to confer legal, material, and emotional benefits for the revolution. The conclusion discusses the impact of all of this on women's lives and on the war effort overall, arguing that the viability of the revolution depends on women's ability to care for their community and kin and to determine and (re)imagine their futures.

In examining the relationship between mobilization for the war and the gendered household, this book aims to draw out lessons for other war-affected countries and transitional contexts. Although this particular research is focused on the Kachin experience—and specifically on the period after the 2011 outbreak of conflict in Kachinland—this book asks larger questions about the relationship among militarization, the household, and insecurity that are of relevance for other contexts.

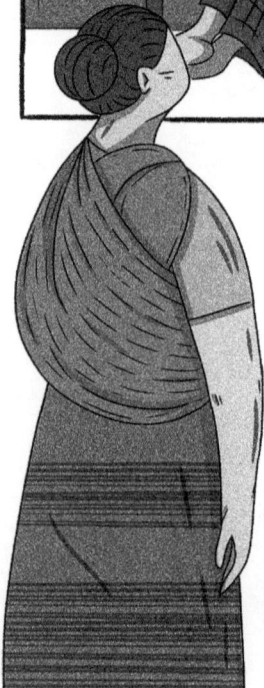

CARE, LOVE, AND DEPLETION IN DISPLACEMENT

I stretch my legs during a lull in the interview with male land mine survivors, all former soldiers and commanders in the Kachin Independence Army (KIA). The men we speak to are tired and need to take a break. Their wounds are infected, and the two men in their midtwenties, who have lost their eyes and part of their hearing, shuffle around on the bench they sit on, waiting for help from their wives, as they cannot move around on their own.

Their wives, however, are busy cooking. Thankfully, the spicy smell from the kitchen masks the much stronger stench emanating from the pigsty behind us where the wives are running a small pig farm. Walking here, I noticed the vegetable patch they are working on, growing food for their families. Outside the kitchen, several rows of clothing have been hung out to dry. Children are running between our legs, occasionally falling over in their curiosity to take a closer look at the foreigners in their midst.

One woman comes over to clean her husband's wounds. She grabs the shoulder of one of the children and, at the same time, wipes the child's nose with the end of the sweater. When I ask the land mine survivors how they make an income, they respond that they don't, but their wives do: their wives sew jumpers to sell and walk to the KIA office down the hill twice a week to pick up their ration of rice. Slowly taking in the scene—the pigs to feed, the children to watch, the men to nurse, the clothes to wash, the jumpers to be made and sold, the vegetables to be grown—it suddenly strikes me: without these women, these men would not make it through the week, nor could the military itself survive.

As the vignette recalls, in 2016, I spent time in the KIA's Third Brigade, an area close to the Chinese border. The nights were cold, and I shivered under my thick blanket, but the days were hot enough to dry chilies and clothes, which women living in the brigade headquarters were busy doing. Driving from the compound I stayed in, I could see Chinese houses on the other side of the river, little red flags attached to their roofs—a precaution initiated after a Myanmar military attack saw bombs dropped on the wrong side of the border. I was in the headquarters to speak to land mine victims, all former soldiers, all men. These men resided on a small hill in the military compound with their wives and children. Two of the men were blind; the third had lost one of his legs. Because of their injuries, the men could not do any physical work or help out around the house. But the women worked. As one man explained: "A lot of my responsibilities as a father I have had to give to my wife—I feel really bad now, very stressed. I ask the hospital for bandages, but other support they don't have."

During the few hours I spent on the ground outside their houses, built wall-to-wall, the wives undertook the following tasks: harvesting herbs and vegetables, drying chilies, cooking rice and vegetables, carrying fuel on their backs, liaising with local army staff about their family's rice ration, washing and mending clothes by hand, and feeding their children. They moved quickly; in the midday heat, they did not spend much time outside in the sun, other than to take in the *longyis* (a traditional skirt-like garment worn by men) that had dried or to grab a child by the collar and ask them to run down the hill with a message or a favor for a neighbor. The kitchen, by far the largest building among the smaller ones the families lived in, was communal and, by the looks of it, heavily used: the walls were sooty from cooking over an open fire, and the dirt floor was leveled almost smooth by heavy use. When I peeked in just before leaving, I saw two of the women bent over four simmering pots. Bundles of pounded, green chilies were on the table. One woman stayed with the men outside to greet several KIA soldiers who had driven up on their motorbikes. The women also took care of their husbands' medical needs, stopping by every few minutes to clean their festering and wet wounds. One of the men told me: "I feel so sorry that I cannot work. I have a family and I can't do anything to support them. I feel so sorry for what I cannot do. My wife doesn't work." He added: "I don't want to talk about my relationship with my wife, but when I got this injury I cannot go back to [live] with my mother because I am blind."

As this man suggests, within the home, women are responsible for ensuring that the needs of both husbands and children are met, yet their reproductive duty is not accepted as "work." Of course, the woman this former soldier referred to, along with the other two wives living in the compound, labored continuously during my interview with her husband: while the men sat for the duration of the interview, the women were always on their feet. In fact, it was my meeting with these women that opened my eyes to the critical work undertaken by women in resourcing armed insurgency groups. Yet the man's expressed sentiment, that his wife did not work, is in line with dominant notions framing women's labor as less valuable and militarized care as incidental rather than central to militarization processes and insurgency warfare. The militarization of caring activities reinforces women's roles as keepers of tradition and culture at the same time as it results in wives and mothers taking on unwaged positions as caretakers of and providers for injured soldiers and veterans (see Tharaphi Than (2014) for a discussion on women's symbolic role in Myanmar).

However, the burden of militarized social reproduction lies heavily on women who do not have the income or the family connections to use the help of women's organizations (discussed at length in chapter 2). None of these women had access to a nursery school, and, apart from their rice rations and their housing, they did not receive help from the KIA. One of the injured men told me: "We are a weak organization, we don't have enough [weapons] or soldiers. . . . We can't complain." His wife was more vocal: "At first, I was so stressed and worried. Before the accident, we were going to apply for him to leave the KIA and go back home. Now we can't go back home—there are a lot of Burmese in Myitkyina, and he still has shrapnel in his leg. I need to work to get money." Militarized care is here tied up with the need to generate income and ensure that not only are bandages changed and wounds kept clean but also that everyone has enough to eat and live on. But therein lies the paradox: at exactly the time when the need for this labor increases, the possibility to engage in it decreases. The more women have to take care of everyone else, the less they can provide for them materially.

As the 2014 Myanmar Population and Housing Census shows, with labor force participation dropping steeply among women with children at the same time as poverty increases, women must often leave paid work in order to provide the social services that do not exist in Myanmar today: caretaking, nursing, and looking after children and the infirm. Tellingly, data from the census reveals that 79 percent of women who report being "economically inactive" in Myanmar are in this category due to household responsibilities. This can be compared to a mere 9 percent of men reporting economic inactivity due to household work. In Kachin State, less than half of all women surveyed were formally employed, compared to 83 percent of all men, although *three-quarters* of these women worked without pay on farms and in the household (Myanmar Department of Population 2016).[1] While the census did not reach liberated areas, similar patterns can also be observed in Kachinland, where the return to outright hostilities has put further strain on the ability of the Kachin Independence Organisation (KIO) to provide social services and, therefore, on women to provide for their families.

As a member of the KIO Central Committee told me with a regretful shrug of his shoulders when I met him in Laiza in 2018: "Before the war we had our policy where if both partners in the family, husband and wife were both service providers, or members of the KIO/KIA, then we would provide food necessities to every single family members. . . . But after 2011 we find it difficult, because of the extra cost of the war." It is not just the KIO/KIA who find this difficult, however. The wife of one of the injured men said: "We didn't have enough money for him to go to [China for health care]; the KIA didn't give us any money to go. So we had to borrow money from others to go. I was so upset and stressed."

While the KIO's health department operates both hospitals and health centers able to treat common ailments and diseases, the resumption of the conflict in 2011 meant that several clinics operating out of Shan areas had to close, and in 2020, the KIO reported having its COVID-19 checkpoints attacked by government forces.[2] Moreover, even if health care exists, complicated surgeries and cases must be referred to hospitals across the border in China; access to those medical opportunities is reportedly expensive, and, therefore, as the wife notes, out of reach for most people. The solution: women's labor, which here not only sustains the individual soldiers; it also helps prop up the gap in welfare by, in effect, enabling the armed forces to divert their funding elsewhere. One man, an adviser to the KIO, explained: "We don't have a proper welfare system for the soldiers. They only receive 10,000 MMR but they don't receive this every month. Maybe they receive this every three months, so it's very hard for soldiers to survive. Also, they don't get food so it's hard. If they have a family, then they can send [supplies] but if they don't have a family they cannot survive."

As the circumstances of the land mine victims and their families illustrate, women's labor is essential for ensuring that the material and emotional needs of families and husbands are sustained. This also ensures that the sacrifices required of the (male) soldiers are not forgotten or made in vain. As one of the husbands mentioned previously reminds us: "I was fighting, yes—not only for the KIA, but for the survival of our nation." His wife, at the time of the accident two months pregnant and with a toddler, adds that although they struggle for income and often quarrel now: "I encourage him, I say 'I am your leg' and try to comfort him." Thus it is not only the sacrifices of men but also the labor and love amassed by wives and mothers, and the exhaustion and depletion that this results in, that go into forging both affective and material ties to the nation. This labor is particularly urgent in areas under the control of the KIO/KIA where protracted displacement and ongoing conflict, alongside the targeting of health systems, have resulted in women having to shoulder the responsibility of maintaining everyday life for the injured and the ill. Yet in displacement camps run by the KIO, where the majority of the residents are women and their dependents, the situation is desperate, profoundly unsettling the ability of the household to reproduce the revolution.

Militarized Social Reproduction in Displacement

The provision of militarized social reproduction is bound up with the changing dynamics of the conflict and the broader needs and effects of the war. This is not a static process but rather a dynamic one—a fact that is perhaps most evident in the displacement camps to which people have fled after losing their land. At the time of my last visit to Kachinland, just over one hundred thousand people resided in displacement, and they were scattered across close to two hundred displacement camps, ranging from smaller makeshift camps and ad hoc shelters in church buildings to larger camp settings with thousands of residents. Around 40 percent of the displaced population lives in areas controlled by the KIO; it is to these areas that the Myanmar government, since 2016, has restricted international aid from reaching those most in need, leaving camps dilapidated and run down.

In 2013, I first visited displacement camps located in liberated areas. When I returned in 2016 and again in 2018, the camps were still there, their blue corrugated roofs glimmering in the afternoon sun, but the obstruction of humanitarian aid had left its mark: most of the houses I visited were drafty lean-tos that did not provide much shelter from the cold winds. Walking on the makeshift roads within these camps, my sandal-clad feet would soon take on a reddish hue.

Several of the women I interviewed had been displaced more than once after attacks on their camps, including shelling by Myanmar military forces. A 2021 report by the UN notes that the protracted nature of displacement—with many households having been cut off from regular access to land, livelihood opportunities, and health services since the outbreak of fighting in 2011—is driving especially high levels of vulnerability, insecurity, and depletion (UNOCHA 2021): in short, the situation in these camps is desperate.

Two women I met in 2018 taught me what militarized social reproduction looks like in the camps. They both lived in a camp run by the KIO; when I visited, it was winter, and the ground we sat on was chilly despite the mat that was laid out. The air around us smelled like burned plastic; tender greens grew in plastic bottles strung off the walls. I learned that they had eleven children between them, ranging from a newborn to sons old enough to serve in the KIA. One woman's husband was in the KIA; the other woman was a widow. The toddlers were running between us, some of them lacking underpants or socks despite the chill. The baby, lying on the ground next to his mother, was sick with cramps and diarrhea, which the mother kept wiping away with an old rag, explaining that it was difficult to access communal water. The mothers made a precarious income from pig farming, which they sometimes supplemented by weaving traditional bags: both examples of livelihood projects initiated by a local community-based organization in an attempt to help displaced women and their families make ends meet. The bags did not sell well, however, and pig farming required the women to leave the camp. Still, they were grateful for the income, small as it was, saying that "it's not improving our lives, but it helps us breathe again."

Though neither of the women had finished school, they both kept meticulous track of the money they made from their livelihood project. While rubbing the stomach of the sick baby, the younger of the mothers explained that "since we don't have men here to build the pig houses, we have to do it or pay someone else to do it." To afford this, they would harvest sugarcane or work on the banana plantations, sometimes enlisting older neighbors to help take care of their toddlers when they were out in the fields, often getting up at 5:00 a.m. to start the day. They also had to pay for education-related costs: for the younger children, this included school bags, uniforms, and umbrellas; for the older ones who went to school in the nearby city, this included school fees. And like many other women I spoke to, these women also provided direct financial support to cover the basic living costs of male recruits.

The younger woman, the one with the baby, told me: "I have five children and a husband. I am the breadwinner in this family, as my husband is in KIA." When I asked if she supported her husband with anything, she started laughing. "Yes, everything!" I learned that she sent him phone money, medicine, petrol, shorts, slippers, and underwear. "I even bought him a motorbike," she said, still smiling at my naivete. "I also need to support my parents, but I don't give them money, but curry or sugar or milk, things like that." The older woman explained that she also supported the soldiers in her family: "My two sons are in the military, but they stay in the mountain so they don't earn money. I support them with everything! Motorbike, phone money, soap, flip-flops, toothpaste, fuel, boots and phone, everything. I support them with everything but the uniforms."

As these experiences show, even displaced women—just barely surviving on a combination of food aid, livelihood assistance, and casual day labor wages— are situated as being responsible for the maintenance and reproduction of the military household. But the women are not just sustaining their families; the army is also dependent on their direct material support. These needs are compounded because, within the Kachin army, salaries are low, almost nonexistent, for low-ranking soldiers. As a result, female soldiers, as well as the wives and mothers of soldiers, are tasked with maintaining the survival of the household through precarious and often exhausting work. In Je Yang, the largest camp in Kachinland, with almost nine thousand residents, the women's committee targets programming toward helping the wives of KIA soldiers, explaining: "We give priority to the wives of KIA soldiers. . . . The wives of KIA soldiers face huge financial difficulties because their husbands cannot come home and help them. So, we provide this sewing training program to help them earn money by making clothes." An adviser to the KIA, a young man I met in Laiza, told me over dinner in 2018: "Because when you work for the KIA, it's a sacrifice, you work for your country, but the KIA, they can't even support their soldiers." He gestured with his chopsticks at the bowls of rice and greens lining our table. "It's a challenge to get even food and rice for the soldiers, so they can't support the family members of the soldiers." This challenge is shared by women living in displacement.

Over 80 percent of people living in displacement in Northern Myanmar are women and their dependents. When I arrived at camp settings—I visited six in total, one in government-controlled area, the other five in liberated areas—men were not visibly present. Instead, I saw younger children running between houses and women tending to their households. A woman with seven children and a sick husband living in a small camp run by the KIO, located just a couple of kilometers away from the brigade headquarters explained: "There are not many men here—many are military servants [soldiers], and many more are unhealthy. So most families rely on the mothers to provide." Her friend, an older woman with small amber stones in her ears, remarked that "living in the camps is not comfortable. . . . We have poor health and my children have no education. But we are trying to bear it—we remind ourselves that this is for the future of the nation." The material and affective ties among the household, the displacement camp, and the army are in this way steeped in notions of duty and gendered relations of care and realized through difficult and, at times, backbreaking labor.

Precarious Work and Land Loss

In militarized care, subsistence and reproductive work are blurred. Women produce material and emotional sustenance to the individual soldiers, the household, and the war machinery at large, but the struggle to do so is made almost impossible by the loss of property, land, and home, which pushes women into precarious labor. Forced into displacement after fleeing attacks, many, if not most, of the families I spoke to were unable to return to work on their land. Indeed, in most areas touched by the war, access to land had been effectively cut off by the fighting, with fleeing families having to leave their farms behind (UN Women 2021). "When we ran," a group of displaced women I met in Mai Ja Yang in 2016 told me, "the Burma army burned down our village. We are afraid to go back; there are landmines everywhere."

The intensification of the conflict in Kachinland has then resulted in not only widespread displacement but also extensive land dispossession. A UN report from 2018 shows that 84 percent of displaced people surveyed had no documentation to prove ownership. Land left behind has reportedly been appropriated by armed actors and business interests that are usurping land for commercial purposes. Indeed, according to Human Rights Watch (1992), large tracts of land have been sold to Chinese companies for the purpose of developing banana plantations.[3] The same women quoted above explained: "If we go outside [leave the internally displaced persons' (IDP) camp], it's more difficult to live. We don't have any money, and if we go outside we don't have a home or land. . . . Now we work on the sugar plant." Virtually all of the displaced women interviewed for this book, *if* they had paid employment, worked as day laborers cutting sugarcane or harvesting bananas, sometimes on the very land that had previously been their communal land. One of the women I met in Mai Ja Yang, a quiet young woman who kept fidgeting with her bag, letting her friends answer the questions, turned to me at the end of the interview. "Everything," she said, "everything we have has been destroyed."

Yet it is in this very environment that women have to try to make ends meet: removed from their lands and their homes, women have to turn to precarious wage labor. Militarized social reproduction is here more than just physical caretaking: it is ensuring that children have food to eat, that injured husbands have access to treatments, that families have heating and clothes. Another woman I spoke to, living in a displacement camp with three children, told me: "We have enough just to cover kitchen needs—we get support from the [camp] committee and [Karuna Mission Social Solidarity] with rice, oil and salt. But this food doesn't come regularly, sometimes we don't get anything for a month. When we don't get anything, we work as daily laborers—like in the sugar cane field, or selling vegetables for people inside the camps." An interview with a camp committee member in Je Yang camp echoes this: "The work in the camp is not regular. This is the most difficult situation right now."

In every camp I visited, women were hard at work collecting firewood, cleaning clothes, tending to pigs, cutting sugarcane, and harvesting bananas, but they received little, if any payment, and always less than men. This was evident in almost all of the interviews I undertook and was also substantiated in a 2020 study showing that displaced women earn up to 20 percent less than men (see Durable Peace Programme Consortium 2020). A group of displaced women I met explained: "Yes, we get less money when we work as daily laborers. . . . When we work in construction, and we carry the big things, we only get 4,000 kyat but a small boy gets 5,000 kyat, even though we can work more than the men." The inequality in pay and this gendered division of labor were corroborated across interviews, and they contribute to women's poverty. This economic vulnerability is compounded by the impact of the war and a growing need to resource families and soldiers.

Problematically, the ability to provide for members of the household becomes more difficult the bigger the family: a 2020 study from the UN shows that poverty rates in Myanmar increase rapidly with the increase in the number of children in a household: nine in ten poor households are households with children [Central Statistical Organization (CSO) UNDP and World Bank 2020]. A young widow living with her four children in a small displacement camp in a government-controlled areas explains this conundrum: "If I bring my children, I can't work. My children are very young, so I don't get chosen [to work]." Another woman, living in Je Yang, shared her experience: "As a mother, I don't have many choices for earning extra money. When I think about leaving the camps to earn money, or crossing the border to work, I remember that there is no safety or security for women. But it's possible to go to the banana fields to work as daily labor—but the money we get from that is not enough to support a whole family."

Women's overwhelming responsibility for their families and the soldiers in their midst is not a new phenomenon. Indeed, women, positioned as de facto heads of households, have had to shoulder critical social reproductive roles in meeting the needs of both their immediate family and the army, without which neither would survive, across cycles of conflict and in the face of state violence and repression. Among my research participants whose parents were working or who had worked as soldiers in the KIO/KIA, all reported that their mothers either had to retire upon marriage or stay in the army while engaging in subsistence production alongside army assignments. This enabled their husbands' military participation and kept their household alive. A quote from a woman who joined the uprising in 1962 and ended up working as a medic until she got married seven years later is illustrative of this. After her marriage, her family separated as her husband worked actively as a soldier and she stayed behind to take care of the children: "I had to take care of my family and children because my husband had to stay in military camps. So, I often stayed behind in a village with my children and worked in a farm [slash-and-burn farming] to feed my family. My children were young, but I had nobody to help me take care of them when I went to work at the farm. So, I put them inside the house and locked them up with some food for the day, so that they would not go out."

Like many other women with husbands stationed with the army, injured in the war, or deceased due to conflict, disease, or substance abuse, this former soldier ended up being the de facto head of her household, engaged in subsistence work to make ends meet. As of this writing, among the women I met living in displacement, daily wage labor has replaced the collective farming and work on lands that used to be done in the villages predisplacement. While this enables women to meet the immediate needs of their families through precarious and underpaid work, the intensification of these needs alongside untreated trauma and diseases may also lead to bodily and emotional exhaustion.

Feminist research has demonstrated that it takes time to make life meaningful, that the efforts involved in making ends meet—the mundane repetition of everyday life, especially when this work is not valued or recognized—deplete and tire out the very bodies involved in this labor (Gunawardana 2016; Rai, Hoskyns, and Thomas 2014). It is labor that is felt and experienced in and through bodies, leaving women physically bearing the burden of doing too much. As I have explored in this chapter, this is especially the case in times of conflict. Yet this is also labor that sustains traditions, identity, and knowledge across generations: a labor of love and duty that, in the words of Hilary Faxon (2020, 81), "weave[s] together families and land." This form of reproductive labor becomes even more important in the midst of conflict and upheaval: gendered relations of care and commitment are essential for fostering and rejuvenating the fabric of everyday revolutionary life. But the ability of women and the possibility to do this labor diminish with the demands and the onslaught of the war.

Recognizing the bodily and emotional dimensions of the political economy of war means redirecting the gaze from the battlefields and the soldiers to the land, homes, and families sustaining the war effort through a complex mix of love, duty, and sacrifice. "I love people here. The things that I want to do for them, the things that I want them to get is a lot. I have a spirit that it is okay if people are not hungry even though I am hungry," one of very few female camp-in-charges I met told me. Militarized social reproduction is here clearly more than just changing bandages or cooking food; it is labor tasked with, literally, reproducing the nation through labor centered on the household. Consider the experience of the wives of the injured soldiers or, indeed, any of the women I met in displacement camps. Their labor, embroiled in broader revolutionary fervor and commitment, is essential not only for upholding the armed forces but also for fashioning ties among the new home, the broader ethnic nation, and the army itself. Rising before dawn, they work on banana plantations, sugarcane fields, and in construction. They raise pigs, collect firewood, and carry water. They change dressings, clean wounds, and send money to the front line. In the midst of war, they make sure that the soldiers have not only a home to fight for but a home to return to. However, without opportunities for nourishment or rest, or indeed recognition, this is labor that also frequently depletes and exhausts the very bodies tasked with reproducing life and homes across generations and spaces: with the Kachin armed forces unable or unwilling to pay for their work and the Burman state effectively cutting off aid in the midst of widespread repression and violence, women are left shouldering the needs of their communities. In short, it is precisely when this labor is needed the most that it becomes all but impossible to provide.

Depletion and Militarized Social Reproduction in Displacement

The uneven and difficult demands of wartime survival have made it harder and harder for women to provide for their families.[4] Indeed, the absence of adequate and regular aid to these camps, exacerbated by the obstruction of international aid and attacks on IDP camps by the Myanmar military, has all but unsettled the ability of women to generate an income and survive.[5] A woman with four children who had been living in displacement since early 2011 with her young family told me: "I feel hopeless. I have no hope. I don't know how to stay alive."

Among the women I met living in displacement or in the army brigade headquarters, both the scope and the intensity of social reproductive and productive labor have been affected by the conflict and the new household arrangements they find themselves residing in. Here, ongoing trauma as well as underlying and untreated diseases and illnesses means that the women I met often looked physically exhausted: tired, skinny, drawn. It is clear that the pressure of this labor curtails dreams and hopes and leaves women feeling depleted: "We feel empty, we don't have anything," explained a younger woman in 2016 whose husband was away fighting for the KIA and who was living with her children in a displacement camp. Women's ability to provide for their families is obstructed by the realities and legacies of war, including soldiers, checkpoints, and land mines that expose them to harm and injury or physically prevent them from providing for their families. This in turn leads to further economic insecurity. A woman who fled her home and her land in 2011, leaving all her valuables behind when she ran with the younger of her four children on her back, explained: "I've been back to my village three times, but my home is destroyed. We're not allowed to visit our village again. It's not safe; there are still Burma army soldiers there."

Extensive responsibility for caregiving does not only result in emotional and mental insecurities; it may also increase women's mortality rates due to the physical and psychological burden this entails (Li and Wen 2005). Apart from direct threats from military actors and weapons, frequent pregnancies, miscarriages, births, and breastfeeding further exhaust women's bodies, especially when these women are engaged in heavy labor such as carrying fuel and water on their backs, working in the fields, cutting sugarcane, or harvesting bananas.

An interview with health providers from a women's organization that runs mobile clinics in some of the camps highlighted this: "Mothers are badly affected—when they need to get money they have to work, harvesting sugar cane. Sometimes they breathe in fertilizer, and pregnant women must get abortions. Some mothers give birth within six or seven months, and the children die." They explained that "the problem is that people cannot afford contraception. . . . Sometimes a woman has a newborn baby, and one month later is pregnant again. . . . There are also many cases of deaths of children under the age of five."

Reports by local civil society organizations found women with visibly prolapsed uteruses and other reproductive health problems, some associated with malnutrition and the absence of clean water, others with botched attempts at getting abortions or births gone wrong (see Gender Equality Network 2013). The health care providers quoted previously also pointed to structural issues in accessing health care for women: while most camps in liberated areas have some sort of health clinic supported by the KIO, these clinics tend to be "just for fevers and pains." Therefore, for emergency cases such as high-risk pregnancies, "there is not enough equipment and not enough physicians. So we have to refer to the China side. . . . But we do not have any emergency case referral costs, so it's very difficult for us. For example, when there is a high-risk pregnancy we have to choose—the life of the mother or the life of the child." Another health care worker I spoke to echoed these sentiments: "Abortion problems also occur more than necessary because unwanted pregnancies have increased. For the women in the camps it is hard for them to receive proper treatment regarding pregnancies if they have problems because they have a lack of income so they don't want to go."

This shows how chronic economic insecurity as a direct consequence of displacement, alongside the absence of a welfare net resulting in women compensating for the lack of social infrastructure during and after conflict through unpaid or underpaid militarized care, has disastrous consequences for women's and girls' physical and mental well-being. One woman I met said her head hurt; she hit the side of her forehead repeatedly as she told me this. Another explained how she wakes up with nightmares every night. An older, quiet mother of seven told me that fear affected her ability to speak or listen to Bamar, the language spoken by the ruling elite in Myanmar and by soldiers: when she hears Bamar, she wants to run to the forest with her children to hide from attacks, as she has done many times already. One time, her two older children got separated from her in the chaos that followed an attack. She did not find them for two days. In this way, wars linger in bodies and minds, shaping lives long after the immediate end of attacks, compounded by the reproductive work women are pushed into.

Militarized care here emerges from duty and love as much as from immediate needs and ideological commitments. As the women discussed in this chapter tell us, this is labor that shapes and maintains intimate bonds and relationships both outside and inside of army life, enabling the revolution to continue forward despite the superior strength of the Myanmar military—but often at high costs for the women themselves.

THE POLITICAL ECONOMY OF THE REVOLUTIONARY HOUSEHOLD

Life Story: Seng Raw

I was 16 when I joined the KIA [Kachin Independence Army] in 1963. It was really the beginning of the KIA revolution. I was excited to go. When I first arrived, I was assigned to work at the office as a clerk. They told me that they would provide me training to learn necessary skills to become office staff, but I was not interested in working in an office and also did not have the relevant education. So, I just chose the medical training.

At that time, we used tactics of guerrilla warfare. Mostly, it was male soldiers who went to the frontline, ambushed or attacked outposts of the enemies, while women remained behind and performed other duties. Our leaders talked about the importance of women, but we were not allowed to go to the frontline.

As paramedics, we faced lots of difficulties [challenges]. The women section [camp, column] was a little far away from the main military camp where male soldiers were stationed. At once, my colleague (a woman medic) and I went to the main men's camp to take care of a wounded soldier. We were escorted by two male soldiers. Unfortunately, we encountered Burmese soldiers on our way to the men's camp, and they shot at us. Us women did not have weapons, so I pretended to be dead. Then, the two soldiers who were escorting us shot back at them [the Burmese soldiers], so I gathered my strength and ran again until I found a place to hide and finally we managed to reach to the men's camp and were able to provide medical care to the wounded soldiers.

There were so many times when we were starving, we did not have enough food to eat. Several times we survived by just eating the stem [core/heart] of banana trees from the jungle. We did not have enough clothes either. The weather was terribly cold but we did not have any warm clothes. Sometimes, we took off clothes from the bodies of dead Burmese soldiers and wore them because we could not get new clothes. At that time, only senior leaders or high-ranking officers could wear well-suited uniforms. For ordinary soldiers like us, we did not have proper uniform.

Oh, I have endless stories to tell you, if I talk about my experience in the KIA. . . . After I got married, we faced immense difficulties. We were also on the run as the Burmese army always came and attacked us. Once, we were almost captured by the Burmese army. After that, my husband was assigned to the First Brigade and the family moved along with him. After some years serving with the First Brigade, my husband was transferred to the Third Brigade, and later on he was assigned to the KIA general head-quarters. After my marriage, I had to take care of my family and children because my husband had to stay in military camps. So, I often stayed behind in a village with my children and worked in a farm [slash-and-burn farming] to feed my family.

When I was a soldier, I did not know much about women and gender issues. I had no idea and never heard about any women movement. But, around 1984 when I was with the First Brigade in the northern areas, I was instructed from the KIO [Kachin Independence Organisation] Central Committee to set up a women organization. Since I did not have experience, I did not know how to start organizing a women association, and what would be its activities. But, we were empowered by the leaders, who told us that we [women] were equally capable as men; so we [women] must also participate in politics, as equals of men. So, we started that women organization with the objectives set out by the KIO Central Committee.

The written letter from the Central Committee also included general guidelines for activities that the women organization should carry out, includ-ing health and education for children, opening nursery schools in villages, helping families in need and supporting Kachin politics. So, we started the Kachin Women's Association (KWA) with the guidelines formulated by the Central Committee, although we did not have much experience. Since we did not have funding to run the organization, we collected 5 Kyats from each woman of our movement and started our activities. Our first activity was to welcome KIA soldiers coming back from the frontline with sticky rice and Kachin traditional rice wine. We then tried to raise fund, but it was not easy because money was so scarce by that time. So, we [from the women's group] worked as paid laborer (2 Ks per person a day) in farms of families who need help. We used the funds we raised for our organization's activities.

Serving as a KIA soldier opened my eyes and changed my views. After joining the KIA, I learned about the situation of our people through the patriotic speeches delivered by our leaders. The leaders also told us how important our struggle was, and how important our contributions were to the freedom of our people and [Kachin] nation. That is how I came to know about the oppression and the violation of our rights by the Burmese people. We were lectured to be brave, patriotic and serve for our people and our [Kachin] nation to the best of our ability. After receiving training, I came to understand the necessity to work harder. I have become much tougher emotionally and could speak louder.

Through my involvement, I wanted to achieve independence for the Kachin state. We have been oppressed and our rights have been deprived by the Burmese people. So, I wanted to get an independent state for the Kachin people, in which we can live peacefully and exercise our rights freely. You know, the purpose of KWA was to develop the capacities of the woman, to support their families, to provide health care and education and to encourage them, counsel and take care of the combat soldiers when they return. But gradually, we started to realize that we [women] can play a very important role in the community. We can do a lot. We have the equal capacity to do everything.

What did the outbreak of war mean to ordinary women in Kachinland, and how was the household expected to contribute to the war effort across different cycles of the conflict? In chapter 1, I introduced the concept of militarized social reproduction. In this chapter, I will zoom out and offer a historical perspective on how women's wartime labor—in and outside the household—has adapted in relation to changes in the conflict. In particular, I am interested in exploring what the establishment of a women's organization, the Kachin Women's Association (KWA), meant for women's participation in and experience of the war. To grasp how and why women like Seng Raw, whom we met above, became involved in the broader war effort, moving from soldier to wife to KWA member, we need to understand how an overarching gendered division of labor influenced women's responses to the war, enabling them to contribute to resistance activities in particular emotional, material, and symbolic ways.

Seng Raw's story, along with countless others, illustrates how women have held critical roles in sustaining and shaping the political-economic infrastructure of the KIO/KIA since the outbreak of conflict in 1961. While involvement in the KIA exposed women like Seng Raw to new ideas about politics and nationalism, their participation was premised on a gendered division of labor, which reinforced their maternal, nurturing, and more "traditional" roles while in the armed forces. The establishment of the KWA, alongside the intensification of fighting, prompted a shift in how women contributed to the war by promoting the mobilization of women in a more organized manner, under the direct guidance of the KIO. This suggests that the "cooking, combat, and care" carried out by women both within and outside the framework of KWA played a significant role in sustaining not just the individual soldier but also wider Kachin rebel objectives.

As Seng Raw's story shows us, opportunities for women's direct or indirect involvement in armed struggle have not only changed in response to changes in the war; they have also changed in response to a woman's life stage and social position. This points to the ways in which notions of gender difference have persisted across time, often shapeshifting to accommodate women's changing roles, ensuring that women provide for the army across different life stages. Indeed, a retired colonel, one of the founders of the KIA, told me in 2015 in response to my question as to why more women are not found in leadership within the KIA/KIO: "The reason is [women's] own concept. . . . Women are not in leadership because they become family members." Women, apparently, want to be mothers first and soldiers second, thereby justifying the exclusion of women from leadership opportunities. As the quote from the retired colonel illustrates, women's relationship to and experience of the army and, by extension, political violence, have been structured by an understanding of gendered roles as centered on the household: women are caretakers, first and foremost. Thus, while men have been expected to be frontline soldiers, female soldiers have instead been treated as the exception rather than the rule, responsible for maintaining the home front through their work with the KWA rather than defending the front line. Importantly, the establishment of the KWA suggests the recognition of the critical role played by women's labor in resourcing the war and shows just how seriously the military leadership has taken the reproductive duties of women in Kachinland. With the foundation of the KWA, gendered relations within the individual household, far from being a private matter, became formally enmeshed in the objectives of the military. Indeed, these gendered dynamics helped facilitate the remobilization for conflict, with profound impacts on women's insecurity both after and before the breakdown of the ceasefire in 2011. This suggests two things: that militarized social reproduction adapts and responds to changes in circumstances, and that the importance of women to provide for those affected by fighting—with armed means if necessary—forms a critical component of rebel wars.

Drawing on interviews and secondary sources, this chapter explores the attempt by the Kachin leadership to shape and benefit from a Kachin gender order through the harnessing of women's gendered duties in support of military objectives. My material suggests that after the commencement of the war in the 1960s, and especially at the height of the conflict in the 1970s and 1980s, women's labor became increasingly more oriented toward supporting the needs of warfare in order to achieve the political vision of a self-governing and self-sufficient Kachinland, culminating in the foundation of the KWA. I outline the "herstory" behind the formation of the KWA and the role the organization has played in different stages of the war, examining the ways in which the KWA both provides a platform for women's mobilization to the war effort and circumscribes their involvement. I then look at how changes in the political context after the ceasefire and leading up to the outbreak of fighting in 2011 benefited from a gender order in which women, located at the nexus of production and social reproduction, were positioned as the caretakers of the home and the army.

The Beginning of the War and Gendered Labor, 1961–77

As briefly outlined in the preface, many factors led to the outbreak of fighting in 1961. Though Myanmar had gained independence from the British in 1948, ethnic minority leaders—including the Kachin—felt they were not given equal status in the new country. In 1961, the KIA was established to fight for an independent Kachin state—or Kachinland.

When the uprising began in 1961, women were not allowed to serve formally as soldiers in the KIA. An elderly KWA member I spoke to explained that "in the very early part of the KIO," while women were not allowed in the military training, many young women were in fact very keen to join the army and help out in any way they could, often "helping the army with food making and making clothes, like that, general support." A former soldier who joined a year later, in 1962, recalled that "in the army there were only two types of work for women: we could either work [in] medical care or we could make uniforms." In this way, although only men were officially drafted, women of course participated in the revolution, as remembered by a former soldier and KWA member I spoke to in Laiza:

> From the very beginning of the revolution women was already involved in this process, to help further the revolution. Maybe we are not directly involved in the military but we help the revolution, like dispatching messages because the villages are very far from each other and we don't have any postal service. Usually this was taken care by women because by that time, to travel for a man is very dangerous and risky but for

women we don't have as much risk compared to men. And the women in fact participate in the revolution like that: dispatching mail and postal service and also supplying clothing. Sometimes we make the clothing for the soldiers, but no one ever acknowledged or recognized our support for the revolution.

From the perspective of many of the retired soldiers and elderly KWA members I met, women were as keen as men to realize the revolution, and with armed means if necessary, but the army did not initially provide any opportunities for women to train in combat or even access weapons. The "herstory" of Seng Raw exemplifies women's experiences during this period of time:

Mostly, it was male soldiers who went to the frontline, ambushed or attacked outposts of the enemies, while women remained behind and performed other duties. Our leaders talked about the importance of women, but we were not allowed to go to the frontline. When male soldiers on the frontline got wounded, one or two women paramedics were called to the men's camp to provide medical services to wounded soldiers. The same applied for the cloth-making department: whenever there were new recruits who needed new uniforms, the responsible person from the cloth-making department was called by the male commanding officers to make arrangement for new uniforms. So, women did not have a big role to play in the KIA in the beginning.

These are gendered tasks that have persisted throughout the uprising. When I visited Laiza in 2013, I wandered into an outbuilding adjacent to the KWA office that was stacked with dark green materials waiting to be made into uniforms and caps by young women sitting ready by their sewing machines.

However, not all military women were content with sewing uniforms or being medics. My interviews indicate that the no-women-as-soldiers policy changed sometime in the mid-1960s in response both to demands from women that they be invited in and to the greater needs of the war effort, as this quote by a former corporal makes clear: "I was drafted just after I finished my midwifery training [in 1963]. I used to meet other [KIA] women at the paddy field, and working the field we would talk about our lives, about what we wanted in the future, sharing experiences and things like that. I liked doing that. . . . At that time, we didn't have military uniforms, and us women were not allowed to take military training. It was seen as unnecessary. . . . But we insisted and in 1967 I finally undertook military training; after this, women were also allowed to wear uniforms, which was more comfortable. We could also form a women's battalion." After these demands were levied, women entering KIO liberated territories as soldiers would join the Women's Auxiliary Troops and be allowed to wear both weapons and uniforms. Yet they were primarily assigned roles that reaffirmed their domestic roles, such as nursing and sewing (Sadan 2013, 335–36). Thus, although they were now recognized as formal soldiers, an overarching gendered division of labor still structured their relation to the military. These gendered notions also influenced recruitment strategies: traditional norms around women and motherhood meant that only young and childless women were (supposedly) targeted for recruitment.[1] Once married, women were, with a few exceptions, expected to retire from active duty and instead focus their energies on supporting their families and frontline soldiers.

Gender norms also led to some significant contradictions. As noted above, the first female recruits were not given access to guns, uniforms, or military training despite women's widespread involvement in the revolution. A member of the KIO Central Committee (CC) explained to me that they were too concerned with women's safety to "allow them to enter combat." By invoking a discourse around the defenseless and weak Kachin woman, the soldier, situated as protector of the Kachin community, became automatically gendered as male. Women entered this site as markers of difference, as representatives of a female, domestic sphere, and they were banned from the front line.[2] Yet women participated in the public military sphere and experienced combat. My interview with a retired nurse highlights this contradiction: as a female soldier, she was officially not allowed in combat and not outfitted with weapons, but as a paramedic, she was deployed to the front lines and expected to undertake hard, backbreaking labor: "We were assigned to go with the troops in the frontline and carry medical supplies on our own. . . . No matter how harsh the weather was and how dangerous it was in the battlefield, whether it was day time or night time, if we were told to go, we had to go and perform our duties like combating soldiers. When we were called to carry wounded soldiers away from the frontline or if we were asked to bring the wounded soldiers to hospitals, we had to do so." Despite the fact that women undertook heavy and dangerous labor on an equal footing to that of male soldiers, women's participation in the army was circumscribed by strict gender boundaries. In particular, gendered ideas about masculine militarized duties meant that women's experiences of working on the front line alongside male combat soldiers and their ability to undertake work that was physically and mentally very challenging were not necessarily recognized as such.

Seng Raw similarly recalls an attack on her camp, which forced her to quickly flee together with another female comrade. It was rainy season, and taking shelter under a tree, they hid together "coping with plenty of leeches," not knowing where they were. "The next morning, we saw that our bodies were covered by bloods because of the leeches. Although we removed them, the bleeding could not stop easily."

Meanwhile, women who had no direct affiliation with the military themselves were also conscripted to perform household labor and take part in economic activities to support the wartime apparatus of the KIA/KIO. Kachin State itself accessed only marginal economic benefits from the central state, and there was little or next to no social welfare provision (Sadan 2013, 319). Thus the KIA/KIO recognized the necessity of transforming as quickly as possible from a scattered insurgency to a paragovernment, as Martin Smith (1999) puts it—a shift enabled by a new political-economic model in which women's labor came to play an important role. In this new political-economic model of the Kachin revolution, the KIO/KIA envisioned the village as the smallest unit in the structure, followed by the township, the district, and the division. In order to sustain the security apparatus, the administrators in charge of each of these units were responsible for ensuring that taxes were raised and people recruited for the army (Sadan 2013, 334). Taxes were often paid in the form of rice, which each household had to supply to the army,[3] although as the conflict progressed, jade and opium took on increasingly important roles as sources of funding for the army (Global Witness 2015, 87).

The household, as the central unit in the village, became situated at the center of this political-economic structure, with women's labor helping to underpin the economy of the armed forces. With more and more men drafted into the army, my interviews suggest that the KIO/KIA gradually became increasingly reliant on the unwaged and underwaged labor of women to meet the needs of individual soldiers and the army overall. Women I met would recount trading in jade and opium; operating small stalls selling noodles and other food; and ensuring the survival of their children and close kin through subsistence farming, often being the only responsible adult left in the household with the men off at war. What I discovered was a large area of work mostly unrecognized by scholars writing about the conflict.

A woman featured in Lanau Roi Aung's master's thesis at Chiang Mai University on Laiza is typical in this regard: The woman joined the KIA as a soldier but retired upon marrying her husband, a fellow soldier, whom she moved to Laiza with in the 1960s. There, she became the de facto head of the household and their seven children, as her husband was away fighting. She farmed, sewed, traded, repaired both clothes and houses, and, as if that was not enough, she also ran a voluntary school outside her house, a Bible study class in church, and conducted funerals (Lanau 2009).

Feminist insights from the field of political economy demonstrate how women's gendered duties offset state welfare expenditures by providing a constant supply of underpaid or unpaid labor. Such work is dynamic in nature, adapting to changes in the broader contexts in which it takes place (Federici 2004; Mies

2014). Women's material and ideological support of rebel governance institutions and war, like the woman Roi Aung met or indeed any of the older women I interviewed for this project, thus shifted and changed in response to the broader demands of the war economy in which they lived.

During the height of the Kachin conflict in the 1970s, a large proportion of the population still made their living from small-scale agriculture. As more men joined the army and were killed or injured in action or arrested by Burmese authorities solely on the basis of their assumed allegiance to the Kachin revolutionary cause, the agricultural labor force at the village level in conflict-affected areas became depleted, resulting in women often having to shoulder the burden of sustaining the farms alone.[4] However, Kachin women's access to land and productive resources was, and still is, significantly compromised by the fact that they cannot inherit property or land under customary law. Widows and single-woman-headed households were especially vulnerable to land loss, as deeds usually list men as owners (Kachin Women's Association Thailand 2014).[5] Due to the high number of women living and working in farming communities, the marginalization of women's access to land and property resulted in a heightening of the gendered division of labor within conflict communities.

At the same time, the absence of male household members also meant that women played a crucial role during the conflict in the 1970s in ensuring the survival of their families and, by extension, the local economy. In this context, productive, subsistence, and reproductive work blended together as women tended to farms, babies, and army needs. And while women's labor continued to be a major conduit for the viability of the revolution, the changes in women's status—from soldiers to mothers and wives—meant that the form this labor took shifted slightly. A woman who retired from active duty in 1970 to marry a fellow soldier after seven years in the KIA explained that all of the military families lived together. The husbands were away, leaving the women to care for them remotely as well as their dependents directly through different types of militarized social reproduction, often communally organized: "When I got married, like most of the wives of military [personnel], we formed a village. We stayed together like a village. We all had to work on a farm together, farming rice. . . . Mostly, I had to take care of my family, because my husband was always away in the military camp. . . . Most families live by slash and burn farming. But we couldn't live peacefully, as the Burma Army came to our area often. Sometimes they almost captured us! We had to flee often."

All of the older women I spoke to remembered how frequent attacks would force them to flee with their children and extended relatives, leaving behind the fields and buffaloes needed to produce food. They shouldered a huge responsibility in carefully balancing the safety of their families with the larger needs of their community in the context of increased fighting and poverty. Seng Raw similarly recalled how, after her marriage:

> We faced immense difficulties. We were often on the run as the Burmese army always came and attacked us. Once, we were almost captured by the Burmese army. After that, my husband was assigned to the First Brigade and the family moved along with him. After some years serving with the First Brigade, my husband was transferred to the Third Brigade, and later on he was assigned to the KIA general headquarters. After my marriage, I had to take care of my family and children because my husband had to stay in military camps. So, I often stayed behind in a village with my children and worked in a farm [slash-and-burn farming] to feed my family.

The opening of the Yunnan-Kachin border with China in 1980 facilitated an increase in the trade of minerals, timber, and drugs between Kachin State and the rest of the region (Sadan 2013). Women actively participated in trading, in particular in the trade of gemstones and opium, with the profit partly flowing to (male) leaders in the KIO/KIA. In the recollection of Maran Ja Seng Hkawn, a prominent Kachin politician and daughter of late KIO/KIA leader Maran Brang Seng: "The KIA took one third only if they got valuable things, because this was Kachin land, and they had to pay one-third as tax" (Williams, 2017, 95). Many of the women I interviewed for this research recollected their participation in both cross-border and local-level trade before the ceasefire in 1994, often centered on or around the jade mines at Hpakant, which at the time were mainly managed by the KIO.[6]

In addition to trading, many women I spoke to managed small-scale farms and operated food stalls. Although gender roles changed due to changes in production, the gendered division of labor stayed intact, as women were primarily integrated into this war economy in low-paying and devalued roles. Yet these roles required a great level of perseverance, toughness, and creativity. A young woman I met who had grown up in liberated areas in the 1980s recounted just how hard her mother worked during her childhood years, explaining that she never really saw her father, as he was working for the KIA and only came back once or twice per year. As a result, her mother juggled all sorts of work, from operating food stalls and making tofu to trading goods across the state. But she did not stop there. Her labor, which in this book I call militarized social reproduction, also included caretaking, raising children while on the run, worrying about family far and near, and prepping for attacks: "My mum always had a pack ready: matches, an oil lamp, a big rice pot and some rice and dried soya beans. So when we heard the guns, she just picked up the pack and ran with us. We were always ready to flee. . . . I cannot remember how many times we moved. I just remember that there were no place where we stayed for longer than two months. It was a very hard life, always moving around." This woman's mother also probably engaged in subsistence agriculture and cash crops. This combination of material and emotional labor, arduous and critical as it is, is not paid—and, moreover, it is taken for granted. This is important to note because once reproductive work is assumed to be "a feminine attribute, all of us as women are characterized by it. If it is natural to do certain things, then all women are expected to do them and even like doing it . . . ," as feminist economist Silvia Federici puts it (2012, 18).

In other words, in the context of war-torn Kachinland, these assumptions facilitated a gender order that relied on women taking on unpaid duties and subsistence work in support of their families, their communities, and the Kachin armed uprising. Women's active participation in the opium and jade trade was also influenced by this gender order. There was no social welfare to speak of, meaning that women had to shoulder the responsibility to ensure the survival of their household, not an easy task in the face of sustained state violence and a lack of development. This created a context in which many women would engage in work within and outside the assumed boundaries of the household to keep their families and communities afloat. It was also seen as relatively easier for women to travel compared to men, because men were assumed to be combatants. This enabled women's involvement in trading across conflict areas and borderlines.[7] As a retired colonel I spoke to in 2016 put it, men "were unable to do many things, like [acting as] messengers, and [providing] food and medicine, but the women they supported us. They would support us between the cities and our camps. From the very beginning, they have fought for us a lot."

As these experiences show, the need for the households to provide "manpower" for the army reinforced a gendered division of labor, as it resulted in women taking on increased gendered responsibilities. Whether these responsibilities were undertaken within or outside the household, this labor did not occur in isolation from the armed conflict but rather in response to it. Indeed, as recounted by several of my respondents, as the war intensified and communities fled from attacks, women's obligations deepened, especially among women married to soldiers. Women's resistance labor became so critical that by the end of the 1970s, a women's wing was established to help organize women's militarized social reproduction in support of Kachin rebel demands. In other words, the KIO/KIA did not invent these practices, as this labor and the gendered norms they were based on already existed within Kachin communities, but with the development of the women's wing, the army drew on and made good use of what had been until then ad hoc labor.

The Rise and Development of a Women's Organization, 1977–94

While women's gendered roles in the household had long been used to support the resistance, with the establishment of the KWA in 1977, this support became institutionalized, as the gender labor already being undertaken by women was now formally incorporated into the armed structure of the KIO/KIA.[8] The KWA provided the armed forces with opportunities to harness women's gendered duties in support of militarized social reproduction. It was apparently initiated by KIO chairman Maran Brang Seng, "who proposed to the central committee about organizing the women . . . and . . . we set up the KWA in each KIO division which then were the East, West, North, and South divisions," as an interview I undertook in Laiza with three founding members revealed. They recalled that: "during the seventies, when the late chairman Brang Seng travelled abroad, he realized that in the foreign countries the women have roles and rights, but in our Kachin community we don't have many rights. That is why he proposed to the CC about organizing women so that women should have our rights and roles in the community. The CC discussed this and they agreed to form an organization, and to encourage women to organize as a whole. Since then the Kachin Women's Association started to exist. Brang Seng famously argued that while not everyone can fight, everyone can support the revolution. This included women, as Seng Raw remembers: "We were empowered by the leaders, who told us that we [women] were equally capable as men; so we [women] must also participate in politics, as equals of men. So, we started that women organization with the objectives set out by the KIO central committee." She continued to explain that "the purpose of the organization was to develop the capacities of the woman, to help us support our families, to do health care for our children, and to take care of the combat soldiers when they returned from the frontline. We had to provide care and encouragement and counselling to veterans and soldiers." As this quote suggests, women's everyday reproductive rituals formed a critical aspect of the Kachin conflict, and as pressure on the KIO/KIA intensified, so did the pressure on the women.

The labor women engaged in extended from the household to the armed forces, fulfilling much-needed and essential services to their families and community members. Membership in the KWA was not strictly voluntary, as most women married to a soldier would automatically join the KWA. My data indicates that during the conflict in the 1980s and 1990s, female soldiers and soldiers' wives were tasked with providing food, medicine, and clothes to the army through their activities in the KWA. They would sew uniforms, harvest rice, dig trenches, and engage in subsistence agriculture. Women's unwaged labor helped sustain the material needs of the army but also provided women with a platform for political mobilization, which sowed the seeds of more independent feminist organizing.

Outside of the KWA, women would be tasked with gender-specific duties that aided military campaigns, such as ferrying messages or entertaining soldiers and civilians through participation in the KIO's entertainment activities, which toured the countryside performing revolutionary songs and dances. In responding to immediate needs around them, the women I met, whether as mothers, nurses, soldiers, or KWA members, in effect enabled the KIO to direct its expenditures elsewhere while conferring political legitimacy on active women whose participation, although circumscribed, was nevertheless sanctioned by the leadership.

This seems to have coincided with an escalation of the conflict: in the late 1980s, the KIO lost its headquarters as well as its foreign liaison office. Thousands of people fled the fighting as "the *Tatmadaw* launched its largest operation in years" (Smith 1999, 401). As the conflict intensified, the KIO/KIA were able to more effectively draw on women's labor to provide support through women's involvement in the KWA. Wives and female soldiers were required to stretch their household resources to support the revolution in gendered ways that complemented their husband's army activities, and the role of the KWA seems to have become more pronounced: "During 1987, the war became much more intensified, a lot of heavy military campaigns were launched and we lost our HQ. Most of the civilians and the women went to China to take refuge. By the time the KWA organized [helped] the refugees and produced food for the soldiers on the front line. . . . Also, since then we have been taking care of the children who couldn't go to school because of the war. We began establishing childcare centers . . . and visited the soldiers who had been injured in the war, and provided encouragements."

As the experiences of Seng Raw and the other former soldiers I met in Kachinland illustrate, women have nursed injured soldiers back to life, cooked for frontline troops, entered into "revolutionary marriages," birthed new soldiers, kept families and kin alive while on the run, and fought attacks from the Burmese. Yet women are still seen as an anomaly in the army, expected to retire upon marriage and leave the "real" soldiering to the men in order to support the gendered political economy sustaining the armed revolution through reproductive work. While this labor took on a particular urgency during the war, it also mattered outside of the direct theaters of war. In conflict-affected villages in Kachinland, women's gendered labor was undertaken in response to the greater socioeconomic and political context in which it existed, wartime or not.

The Political Economy of the Kachin Household, 1994–2011

In the household, there is still no peace. We don't feel peace. Even though our KIO leaders made peace, we don't feel peace in our household because of the difficult living conditions.

— Kachin woman interviewed in *Global Witness*, 2015

Upon cessation of the hostilities in 1994, changes in the external socioeconomic and political context in which the army existed impacted the relationship between production and reproduction. The ceasefire agreements resulted in the loss of jade mines and an increase in logging as well as opium and methamphetamine production. Despite these external changes to the household, dominant gendered power relations that had developed to support the military structure during the conflict years continued to inform the location and experience of Kachin women.

This was most clearly illustrated through the work done by the KWA. During the ceasefire years, the organization continued to arrange nurseries for children, medical care for disabled veterans, and fundraising activities. A report that included interviews with women in the KIO/KIA in 1995 records how the KWA took responsibility for arranging sewing projects and fur collection in order to raise funds and make uniforms for the KIO. Although the need to provide for the front line receded, as there were no longer any soldiers stationed far away to send food packages and cigarettes to, women living in KIO-controlled areas still kept busy. The report details the many activities women engaged in *alongside* their work with the KIA as medics or clerks: raising livestock (chickens, pigs, goats, and rabbits), household chores, growing vegetables, managing families, taking care of husbands, shopkeeping, jade trading, and noodle stalls (Project Maje 1995).

Military families experienced the return of the male head of household, as male soldiers returned from frontline army camps to live permanently with their families. Although this should have eased the burden on women to provide for their families, the expansion of the drug trade resulted in an increase in drug use among young men. A lack of health care facilities, alongside the organization of women's duties to engage in affective labor, meant that the majority of addicts would remain with their families, resulting in women caring and providing for disabled veterans as well as addicted sons and husbands. Mandy Sadan (2014) notes that more men died during the ceasefire years than during the conflict years due to their addictions.

During the last few years of the conflict, cross-border marriages had begun to take on a greater significance, developed in the nexus of commodification and tradition, with young Kachin women moving across the border to China as brides to Chinese men (Dean 2005, 817). These marriages provided important income for struggling families yet drew on customary Kachin practices in which the dowry plays a significant part in cementing relationships and kinship ties. After the ceasefire in 1994, the practice of cross-border marriage occurred at a time when safe migration options for women were becoming more limited. The central government restricted opportunities for women to obtain passports or to travel (both within the country and abroad) without a male companion. In rural areas, many women could not access formal ID cards or birth certificates (Belak 2002, 197). These restrictions, together with the need for an income among families struggling with addiction, increased women's vulnerability to unsafe migration practices.

Drawing on a commodification of women's reproductive duties to provide support to both their immediate families and the larger community, the development of the KIO's structure of governance during the ceasefire years led to the further institutionalization of women's duties to support the military. After 1994, the KIO extended its governance institutions, establishing a number of departments responsible for regional and community development, including education, health, forestry, and agriculture, tasked with "uplift[ing] the lives of the people who have been suffering from warfare" (Lanau 2009). Not being in an active war also meant that the KIO was able to direct more funding toward soldiers and their families. A member of the KIO CC told me that before the conflict broke out again in 2011, the KIO would help "active service members" and their children (and extended relatives living with them) with food rations. He added: "But after 2011 we find it difficult, because of the extra cost of the war that we have to fund."

While the support to families and soldiers living in Kachinland was ostensibly financed by the extraction and trading of natural resources found there, as Lanau states, women's underpaid or unpaid labor as teachers, nurses, farmers, mothers, rabbit breeders, and soldiers helped ensure that the gaps in the financing were met, as the examples in the 1995 Project Maje report recounted above makes abundantly clear.

As a result, when the conflict recommenced in 2011, the security apparatus of the KIO/KIA was highly conditioned by and able to draw upon the political-economic order of its past, with women able to quickly respond to the changes in needs, as this female lieutenant I met in Laiza illustrates: "First and foremost, for the family of the KIO/KIA personnel, as soon as the conflict started [in 2011] they had to move their family because of their security. Mostly, the husbands are sent to the frontlines or other places, so women have to take care of their family. This is a big problem. . . . If you have to move with your family somewhere far away to be safe, it will cost a lot of money. This means that women have to do a lot of work to find money for transportation, and so on."

Recruitment and Rebellion After the Reignition of War

Recruitment to the armed forces after the ceasefire in 1994 took on a new urgency in the mid-2000s when Brigadier General Gun Maw and his comrades turned their focus to students as a way to facilitate mobilization and support for the armed cause, which they felt had dissipated during the ceasefire years.

Leading up to the outbreak of fighting in 2011, the KIO had successfully engaged in a range of activities aimed at creating a militarized movement among youth and students to draw upon for support in times of need. While these activities were steeped in the gendered logic of the past—when sons were both the favored and assumed recruits over daughters, as a young female captain I interviewed in Laiza in 2013 reminded me—they were also informed by a greater push from a new leadership to reignite popular support for the KIO/KIA. The 1994 ceasefire, widely perceived to have brought riches to crony businessmen while enabling the Myanmar state to encroach on Kachin territories, eroded the armed groups' legitimacy among both the civilian population and foot soldiers (Smith 2016; Brenner 2019). Scholar David Brenner (2019, 351) argues that the behavior of the leadership and the outcome of the ceasefire deals effectively crushed "the morale within the middle and lower ranks of the KIA," as a result of which their support base crumpled. L Gum Ja Htung (2018, 85) writes: "Therefore it can be said that the previous ceasefire period didn't bring peace, but it enabled the government to implement its statebuilding strategy through the deployment of more troops in conflict areas and granting of economic concessions to ensure the consolidation of territories and resources." This set the stage for a group of younger officers to take charge. These officers included charismatic Brigadier General Gun Maw, who moved up the ranks to hold a variety of important positions within the KIO/KIA's CC. Part of Gun Maw's strategy for reinvigorating support for the KIO/KIA was to focus on university students, whose support had dwindled during the ceasefire years. An older colonel I spoke to in 2014 remembered that "Gun Maw wanted to open the minds of younger generation in university so we can get better leadership in the future."

Education was key to the broadening of the support base for the movement, both *within* KIO-controlled areas and *outside* of these areas. Two notable examples of these recruitment drives include the KIO's youth initiative, the Education and Economic Development for Youth (EEDY) training, which began in 2003, and the National Service program (NS), which began in 2015 and which we will look at in more detail in chapter 3.

However, young women and men can also transition directly into the KIO or the KIA upon graduating from high school. In areas under KIO control, the KIO's Education Department organizes primary through high school education. The curricula used in these schools are similar to the ones used in Burmese schools across the country, with two important differences: since 2011, the history and objectives of the KIO/KIA are taught, and Jinghpaw, rather than Burmese, is the main language of instruction.[9] Upon graduation from high school, students who want to undertake military training join either the KIA officer school, which opened to women around 2009, or the noncommissioned officer school.[10] Willing candidates can also enlist with the KIA directly or attend vocational training (which includes three months to two years of military training) for public service in a KIO department.[11] Like other militaries, while enlistment may be voluntary, postings are not necessarily so. Instead, the military decides where a soldier will work and in what capacity. In 2016, I interviewed a private in the army who had been sent for training with the General Administration Department. Although she wanted to attend the officer training school in Laiza, she was deemed too weak and not fit enough, and at the end of the training, she found herself drafted into a lower-ranking administrative position. This decision was most likely based on both the needs of the army and the war and gendered notions about aptitude, which restricted her opportunities for officer training. And, as in the past, women are restricted to back-office and support jobs, as a man in the CC reminded me when I spoke to him in Laiza. He explained that while the women are "motivated," it is too dangerous and difficult for women to be on the front line. Better for everyone, he reasoned, if women were to support soldiers rather than attempting to be soldiers themselves.

This shows that, while a need for more "manpower" might lead military organizations like the KIO to turn to women, the inclusion of women has resulted in tensions that are "resolved" by preserving some military roles for men, such as combat and frontline duties.[12] Female soldiers need to be "protected," their opportunities curtailed for combat and therefore leadership duties, instead recruiting them into lower-ranking roles that are, above all, temporary to ensure the continued reproduction of the war economy (as we will see in chapters 3 and 4).

Of course, this is not to say that everyone agreed with the demands of the KIO to become loyal and supportive military subjects, or even that all Kachin women participated in the war effort. But the contradictions and conflict that these demands gave rise to reveal the presence of an overarching gender order that structures the possibility for agency, whether in compliance or in rejection. As Seng Raw recalls, mobilization into the KWA, together with her experience of working in the KIA, opened her eyes to political inequality and made her "tougher" as well as more aware of the issues affecting women in Kachinland. In chapters 2 and 3, I will take a closer look at how these contradictions have affected women's possibilities for contestation and political agency both before and after the resumption of the war in 2011, and how this has shaped their participation in the current war effort.

WOMEN'S MILITARY CONSCRIPTION IN KACHINLAND

Life Story: Seng Moon

At the time, I had just finished my midwife training and was waiting for a government post when the Village Defence Force (VDF) recruited me; they sent me to a KIA [Kachin Independence Army] camp. They enlisted me because the KIA needed nurses. The VDF sergeant knew our family; he had already conscripted my husband. The VDF are not the army, exactly, but they know how to protect the village, and how to protect themselves to protect the people in the village.

I didn't really know about the KIA then. I knew they had recruited my husband, and then there was a song which praised the three brothers of the KIA, which made me interested in my heart because I am also Kachin.

When they recruited me, I didn't know what it meant, that we had to stay in the forest, so my family packed a big bag for me, including things for my bed. When the VDF came to take me it was evening time. I felt excited. The next morning, after we had rested, they said to me "Oh this bag, that is useless," so I had to leave the bag behind (laughs).

I was sent to live in a women and children's camp. The women are sewing for the soldiers, and I am working as a nurse. My husband was at the frontline, and then I realized I was pregnant. Oh, when they [KIA] knew I was pregnant. . . . At that time the discipline was very strict. Women and men have to live separately, and so they think I am not a lady. They didn't know that I was married! I told them. They were very angry with me, and I was sent to a village where I delivered my baby son in May.

My husband was allowed back to see his son, but when my baby was one year old he [my husband] died on the frontline. My extended family took the baby, because I had to go to the jungle and a baby cannot live in the jungle. This was very, very difficult so. . . . The army didn't let me go back to my son. Yeah, so . . . very difficult at that time . . . (cries). I . . . sometimes I went to the village and heard a baby crying. That made me so sad. I began to think, "Oh is my son also crying like this?" I was very sad (cries).

At that time I didn't have any military training. I had to carry a basket, and I was also wearing a tameiin, so it was quite difficult to run away from the Burmese soldiers. One day we had to run for the mountain, but the mountain was very, very high and very cold. Because of my clothes, I fell down. I thought, "Oh, this is not comfortable for us. We need army training and we need to have a shoulder bag and the army clothes, like that."

In 1967, I was allowed to do army training. We were only two women in the training. After the training, I stopped working as a nurse, and I begin work in the office, with deciphering. In our culture, they think that women should not fight. Women should only provide support, in the office, or in the hospital or by using the sewing machine, and cooking.

I was in the KIA for ten years. I was a Corporal when I left, but it is hard for women to reach high positions. No women are generals. Women get married and then they leave.

Even after I left, they still wanted me to help them [KIA]. In 1974, I had assisted with some underground activities, and was waiting to go home [resigned], but Burma held elections that year so I couldn't leave. So, they called me and asked "Why are you leaving us?" I said I wanted to go home, and that I had some health problems. "No, you don't go home," they said. They gave me three choices: One, you come and join in the village and help the teacher at school. Two, you come and join the KIA at the trafficking area at the headquarters, or three, you work in Thailand with the underground movement. I walked from our headquarters to Thailand, on foot. It took us three months.

They wanted me to organize logistics and transport between Kachin and Thailand. They think that women can do this more freely: move more freely, to walk back and forth. We carried secret words back and forth. I was afraid sometimes.

In the late 1970s, I helped found KWA. First Breng Seng talks with his wife, and then his wife talks with us about the KWA. At that time we didn't have uniforms, but had to make them ourselves, so the intention [for KWA] was to sew uniforms. But first we had to cook porridge and sell oranges to raise funds to buy the machines! Also we needed to help look after the army families, like when the soldiers are at the frontlines and mother and baby are home.

Although men are working every day in the military, the women are supporting them. Men might get killed on the frontline, but for the women when the men are gone, the women are the ones who need to take care of the children—food, health care, everything for the household, and sometimes they need to run too, so the men . . . even if the men joined the military and if they are killed, the suffering is still left with the family.

Several years ago, I was sitting in the Kachin Women Association Thailand's (KWAT) office, teaching a class on women's rights and global politics when a couple of my students began to talk about growing up in a never-resolved war. They started talking about sisters joining the revolution and brothers going to the theological college. This struck my curiosity, as it was not the usual war story; the usual story is about male warriors fighting to safeguard women, as Jean B. Elshtain (1987) shows us in her classic work *Women and War*.

As I spent more time on the Thai-Myanmar border, I began to wonder about the experiences of other female "revolutionary soldiers" I knew and why we did not hear their stories. One possible answer that presented itself to me as I watched the female students in my midst being tasked with cleaning the offices of mostly male political activists in the aftermath of the annual rainy-season flood, was that the ways in which women are so readily expected to take on caretaking and cleaning duties might obscure their capacity for violence and the political nature of their labor. Indeed, as I began to do research for my thesis in 2015, it seemed as if the ways in which women were recruited for the military, often as a second choice and mobilized into gender-specific roles as nurses, logisticians, and seamstresses, have helped erase their political labor from dominant stories about the war.

This chapter therefore attempts to recover and understand the experiences of military women mobilized for war. While chapter 2 focused on the establishment of the KWA as a way to explore how women contribute to the war effort (both within and outside of the armed forces), this chapter investigates why women are mobilized into specific military roles. I draw here on interviews undertaken with older women who joined the army during the 1960s and 1980s, as well as interviews with more recent (post-2011) graduates of the officer military training program. This allows me to examine how female soldiers experience life in the armed forces, and show the extensive participation of women in the Kachin revolutionary cause across different cycles of war. I find that while women's military participation waxes and wanes in relation to the broader demands of the war effort, women's military mobilization consistently draws on and reasserts a gendered division of labor, which positions women as undervalued and/or unwaged workers largely responsible for the social reproduction of the household and the army. Thus, despite women's involvement in a variety of positions across the armed forces, conversations with female soldiers reveal that women receive consistently lower pay, occupy relatively lower-ranking positions, and are excluded from combat positions, which are a gateway to promotions, as will be explained in more detail below.

In other words, women and men may both experience combat, work as medics, or train soldiers, but women's labor is coded as feminine and therefore valued less. Military labor markets, like civilian ones, are gendered (Duncanson and Woodward 2015; Woodward and Duncanson 2016), and the army is invested in enforcing gendered differences as a way to capitalize on militarized social reproduction.

This gendered division of labor has consequences: while the lack of money makes some women vulnerable to experiencing abuse within the ranks, the absence of women in decision-making positions makes it difficult for them to openly challenge any gender-based discrimination or harassment they face. Just as Martha Akawa writes about the Namibian resistance movement, that the "lack of women's representation in the . . . administrative structures" enabled the violence experienced by women in the South West Africa People's Organisation (Akawa and Gawanas 2014), I understand military women's experiences of discrimination and harassment as an outcome of an unequal division of labor in which the burden of militarized social reproduction is expected to be shouldered by women.

Scholars of state armed forces have noted how military organizations "have a long-standing history of male domination" (Persson and Sundevall 2019, 1040), constraining women's access to combat and officer-level positions. Military service requires sacrifice, not just of bodies but of time and effort, as soldiers are stationed away from home and do not keep regular working hours. Military organizations are in this sense "greedy" institutions (Mady Wechsler Segal quoted in Carreiras 2006, 57). This makes it particularly hard for women to enter military service, as they are expected to (also) take care of the household. Moreover, the coding of military bodies, institutions, and labor as masculine is a key feature of military logic: in military training and through the sculpturing of the body into a fit and combat-ready "war-machine" (Kirby 2020, 223; Stern and Strand 2021), military organizations are expected to turn boys into men, loyal to the national cause (Lomsky-Feder and Sasson-Levy 2015; Sasson-Levy 2002). I expand on these arguments to show how in the Kachin armed forces, such thinking entrenches a gendered division of labor that results in both obscuring the importance of women's military work for the broader war effort and exposing women to discrimination, depletion, and insecurity.

To demonstrate how women's work has sustained the efforts of the Kachin armed forces across cycles of the war, this chapter centers women's military labor in its analysis of militarized social reproduction. This focus allows me to reveal how material and military ties to the nation are forged through women's labor, sacrifices, and dedication. An emphasis on women's work therefore makes possible a new understanding of the mechanisms by which revolutions and wars are experienced as well as reproduced.

A Military Gendered Division of Labor

The exact number of female soldiers in the Kachin armed forces (now as well as historically) is difficult to assess. What is clear, however, is that even though women are recruited alongside men to practically and materially resource the military, women's participation is both contingent upon and restricted by a gendered division of labor. This gendered division of labor distances women from combat and leadership roles; exposes them to economic and physical insecurity; curtails the length of their involvement; and reinforces women's civilian status. And at the center of this are gendered notions concerning bodies and sexuality, which serve to set the female body and its assumed duties apart from the masculine one. The "highly gendered aspirational pledge of military" (Stern and Strand 2021, 2) not only promises to turn boys into men but also inheres gendered ideas about what kind of society one is fighting for—typically one where women are "both the object of the fighting and the just purpose of the war" (Sjoberg 2010, 55, quoting Jean B. Elshtain). Thus, women's inclusion in military matters troubles this dominant war story.

Women and Military Conscription

As the experience of Seng Moon, recounted at the beginning of this chapter, illustrates, women's military conscription has caused the Kachin military a great deal of concern. While the need for more recruits has led the military to (regretfully) turn to women, concerns about the behavior and experience of military women relate to broader issues about women's role in the Kachin nation. Put simply, women must reproduce the nation through social provision and childbirth, and men must be encouraged to defend their women and their homes. So what does women's military conscription mean, both for the women themselves and the military they are serving?

As Melissa S. Herbert (1998, 43), in her analysis of the US military, notes: "Ever since women first entered the military, there have been conflicts over how to manage the fact that they are women." Everything from uniforms to sleeping arrangements to toilets, pregnancies, and periods have been presented as an obstacle to women's full and substantial inclusion. Seng Moon, like all women entering the military in those early, heady days of the revolution, was not given military training or a gun but instead was put in a women and children's camp, tasked with gender-specific duties: sewing, nursing, and presumably taking care of the children living in their midst. Women were separated from men so that no (heterosexual) romantic relationships could develop, and they had to wear their own clothes, as the uniforms were not tailored for women. As noted in chapter 2, although women's physical capacity (or presumed lack thereof) was framed as an impediment to their military service, women were, after much internal lobbying from female soldiers, given access to training in the late 1960s—some years ahead of many Western state forces that restricted women's soldiering until the 1970s (Denmark, Ireland, and Sweden, for example). Yet concerns about women's physical inferiority alongside their assumed reproductive abilities continued to frame both their contribution to military service *and* their distance from it.

Bodies, Biology, and Combat

Military women's bodies, while on the one hand needed to provide important material and practical labor for the military cause in the absence of male soldiers, are on the other hand rationalized as weak and leaky: as ultimately "tethered" to their female biology (Stern and Strand 2021, 8). This gendered logic also serves to obscure the (political) labor that goes into the linking of women with motherhood, making the idea appear natural, apolitical, and commonsense (Åhäll 2012). If it is only natural that women will have children and stay behind to take care of them, then it follows naturally that their bodies—due to these reproductive duties—are too weak to do "real" soldierly duty (see Hnin Wai 2024).

The female officers and soldiers I spoke to, whether they entered the military in the early days of the war, during the ceasefire years, or after the outbreak of fighting in 2011, all described similar reactions to their participation: as too weak to be in combat and too "leaky" to be fighting on the frontline.[1] As a female warden officer I met in Mai Ja Yang in 2016 put it: "It would be difficult for women to go and live in the forest, like when they have their period. How can they be on the frontline then? It would be difficult for them to do this." Women's exclusion from combat—or as female scholars might call it, the last bastion of masculinity—was then largely framed in biological terms: frontline activities, including combat, are seen as dangerous work where (weak and bleeding) women may be harmed.

For example, a young staff sergeant I interviewed in Laiza in 2014 explained that "there are no women in combat because the combat at the frontline is dangerous, so if the female soldiers get involved, the male soldiers may have to take care of them, and so sometimes the female soldiers might drag down the operation." A twenty-four-year old nurse with eight years in the KIA similarly understood women's bodies as a problem for military effectiveness. She said that "women are not strong or brave enough to be sent to the frontline. There will be a women's battalion soon though, but I don't think it is good." When I pressed her on this, she said she thought this because "women are not strong enough, and some women get sick, like women's diseases [periods], and if they are sent to the frontline it will be more difficult for the other soldiers."

Such notions have resulted in female soldiers being framed as a problem for military effectiveness and order, with women relegated from combat and frontline activities. This also renders men as the "natural and rightful protectors of society" as Megan MacKenzie (2015, 1) writes about the US military experience. The following quote, from a member of the KIO (Kachin Independence Organisation) Central Committee in charge of policymaking I interviewed in 2018, is worth excerpting at length because it reproduces these gendered ideas about women's incompatibility with combat, identifying women as that-which-must-be-defended, rather than doing the defending themselves:

> Our female soldiers, they're very motivated, which is understandable given that the grievances are very big, understandable what we've been through, so of course we understand they want to be a part of it when we're fighting, when we're up against a bigger force. But also at the same time, it's one thing to be motivated, but another thing is to do it practically. It's very difficult. What we see in war films about the front line is very different to reality. So rather than discrimination . . . it's more that because we have such few numbers of women in the army, and also in the organization as a whole, that we want to protect them, we don't want to put them through such hardship. Also, regarding the security, because if they go to the frontline when the enemy attacks, they would have to respond too. And it's so dangerous, that we don't want them to go through it.

Yet these women are apparently seen as fit and strong enough to protect both civilian residences and military centers of command. In response to the intensification of the war after 2011, I learned that women are often left to provide armed security for villagers and headquarters. A female commander I met working in Laiza told me that "the women's corps is stationed at headquarters, and our role is to defend the headquarters. There are several defense lines, but women are in the outer defense line." This incongruity—women as both defenders and reproducers—is made possible by a gendered order in which the head of the armed forces directs and controls the coding of work. In other words, although women may wear uniforms and carry guns, they are not combat soldiers but administrative and medical staff with the ability to provide security if pushed. As a retired colonel in the KIO/KIA put it: "Women also have responsibilities, they have a duty to take care of the country. Morally this is important for women. . . . We don't want to leave women behind. They are also important for the national cause. Now men are on the frontline. Women take care of the office, and the staff administration, and even if they stay behind, if the enemy comes, they have the duty, they have the background of the military education, and they know how to shoot the gun."

While female soldiers don the same dark-green uniforms and carry the same rifles as male soldiers, a division of labor is in place to ensure that female soldiers engage in work that emphasizes traditional gendered skills by drawing on women's assumed abilities to resource the armed forces—materially, ideologically, and emotionally. A young sergeant explained that "[Women] mostly work in the health department you know, women are medics, and also work in offices, like the war office and in the propaganda department." After a pause, she added, "Oh, and women also work in the quartermaster departments, where they organize supplies for everyone." Agreeing with this, a quartermaster officer responsible for overseeing the list of supplies sent to combatant soldiers detailed how "female soldiers produce a lot of supplies for the fighting." She explained that "when conflict happens, the male soldiers are sent to the battleground. Most of the office work and control from the rear of the command is carried out by female soldiers." After a while, she added that as women are more patient than men, women are better suited for these kinds of tasks.

These sentiments highlight how a gendered division of work duties in the armed forces is framed as emerging from women's household duties: nursing, caretaking, waiting. As these rely on skills women are supposed to have developed passively within the home, women's army work is not necessarily seen as skilled or technical per se but rather as "natural." In fact, several soldiers interviewed highlighted how women's innate attention to detail made them better suited for office work. A captain in the police department told me with a wry smile: "At least in the office jobs, women are much more focused on their job and much more disciplined and they can accomplish the jobs much more accurately compared to the male because they have much more concentration, much more discipline. In the office, we perform better than the men." However, in recalling the experience of the colonel quoted at the start of this chapter, women do not only outperform men in the office; they are also needed for and work in a variety of positions, just as well as men. Here, a contradiction becomes apparent: despite their allegedly weak and bleeding bodies, female soldiers do undertake security and experience combat. As recollected also in chapter 2, women are on the front line and undertake heavy and dangerous labor alongside men. Female combat experience is, however, *not* recognized as combat duty.

In other words, formal requirements are utilized to ensure that a gendered division of labor is kept intact despite the realities of the war, which put pressure on women to fill more positions within the armed forces. The combat exclusion is, as Megan MacKenzie (2015) writes, a trope and a fantasy rather than a reality: it is not about women *not* experiencing combat; it is about preserving the notion of the miliary as a male sphere, which women are supposedly only visiting. However, fantasies also have consequences.

Within the Kachin army, women's combat exclusion is also important to pay attention to because if you do not have experience of combat duty—or are not formally recognized as having this experience—you do not become a leader. The internal regulations of the army stipulate that experience of combat duty is a requirement for leadership roles. Women are therefore de facto prevented from reaching top positions within the military. The posting of only men to top army positions, the gendered underpinnings of army recruitment and construction of military duty, and the framing and devaluing of women's labor are illustrative of a gendered political economy at work.

These systemic patterns also help guide the internal behavior of soldiers and ensure that female soldiers—although expected to "take care of the country," as the retired colonel above phrased it—are seen as too weak for frontline duty and too inexperienced (or too busy) for leadership responsibility. The following quote from a female lieutenant also illustrates this sentiment: "Both men and women work for the KIO but in the army, men can work much more effectively. Basically women, when they get married and they have children, they cannot work very effectively, they cannot take any active duty in the army because they have to take care of the children. . . . That's why women cannot be very effective in the army and also why women are not in leadership."

Female soldiers are here expected to manage the household and raise children. But increased household responsibilities result in women having less time to participate in political and public life. In this way, the gendered valuing of work and labor restricts women's access to and experience of military leadership. Even if motivated by patriotism and a sense of duty, (most) women will leave the armed forces upon marriage. The symbolic role held by women in ideologically maintaining the boundaries of the military, when analyzed in relation to their restricted inclusion in the military sphere, results in a double bind: women's military labor is necessary to fill the gap left by men, yet women must also stay in the household in order to socially reproduce the nation. These notions reinforce the idea that women's military duties are temporary and gear women's primary responsibilities toward motherhood and wifely duties rather than a military career. As one young corporal I met summarized it: "Well, women have to leave the military when they get married, that is why there are no women in leadership." Men, I was told, get promoted.

It is worth quoting Seng Moon again: "In our culture, they see that women are women. They should not fight. They should only support [men], working in the office, in the hospital, operating the sewing machines, cook food, like that." More recent evidence supports this claim: for example, even though the military opened the new cadet school to women, ostensibly to attract more female officers, women graduating from that school have yet to be promoted to high-ranking positions or combat roles.

Gender, Insecurity, and Rank

Relations of difference are structured not only by a gendered political economy but also by rank. Rank and gender combine with ideas about military labor to structure women's relationship with the armed forces to, for example, ensure that combat is valorized above other forms of soldiering available and open to women. Rank also works to obscure or abstract the array of insecurities and violations women within the armed forces may face. While a military code of conduct, including rules regulating issues around promotion, punishment, and retirement, is in place within the armed forces, there are no female judges. The code of conduct also regulates intimate behavior, including marriage requests and adultery.[2] These are governed by a military court, which metes out punishment and regulates behavior, or, in the case of smaller infringements involving soldiers, the commander-in-charge and/or a committee of elders. An interview with a senior justice overseeing the work of the KIO court in 2019 reveals just how hard it is for women to become involved in legal proceedings: the justice explained that the absence of women in both the formal and customary system is due to the fact that they lack practical experience of working with Kachin customs and legal procedures, but he will not provide opportunities for female graduates of the KIO law school due to "their lack of experience." This circular argument preserves the status quo, skewing rules and regulations away from gender equality by protecting a gendered division of labor that pigeonholes women as potential and actual mothers rather than soldiers.

In the interview, the KIO justice suggests that the worst hazard female soldiers face is "pregnancy out of wedlock"—as opposed to the very real threats of sexual assault, maternal mortality, and actual battle injuries of the same types that men face. Moreover, such representations of the need for female soldiers to reproduce within the confines of the family (as also recalled in Seng Moon's story) highlight the tensions that female recruitment gives rise to and illustrate how the military's rules and regulations help to emphasize the responsibility women hold for socially and biologically reproducing the army.

Thus, even though external demands for more recruits have on the surface altered certain aspects of female military duty, in practice, the gendered division of labor remains, in many ways, intact. Access to the KIO Central Committee is similarly closed off to women, with members of the KWAT complaining to me about what they felt were very opaque criteria for nominations to sit on the committee, arguably the most important decision-making body in the organization:

> There are no women in Central Committee. But now, the notion of 30% of women participation in decision-making processes is very popular. So they may think about reserving 3 seats for women in principle. When people, especially outsiders or foreigners, ask, [the KIO leadership] answer that 3 seats are being reserved for women. . . . Sometimes, we are so surprised when they say 3 seats for women in Central Committee when outsiders ask! We have tried to nominate at least one member to be in the Central Committee. But they keep turning down our propositions. I don't know what the leaders are thinking.

The rejection of female candidates from both the Central Committee and the military court suggests that gendered ideas about aptitude and belonging affect how leadership and authority are defined. These ideas in turn are linked to women's "inability" to engage in combat or to gain substantive military experience (as they, generally speaking, have to retire upon marriage).

And because this gendered division of labor results in construing men as leaders—both symbolically and practically—women's participation in army activities is undervalued as well as underwaged: women's lower-level positions are not paid well, if at all. Lower-ranking soldiers only receive 10,000 kyat per month (about 7 USD at the time of my interviews), and my research found that this stipend is not paid on a regular basis; soldiers may be paid once every three months and must therefore rely on the material support of their families for survival. However, as none of the women I spoke to had spouses sending them money, in contrast to the male soldiers I met, many of which had their wives and mothers provide them with necessities, lower-ranking women become vulnerable to economic insecurity. In other words, this is a gender order that amplifies female poverty at the same time as women's responsibility for maintaining the survival of families increases due to the protracted nature of the war. Indeed, a recent graduate of the office training programs told me: "If I could change things in the KIO, I would want to create more women programs, and help women to earn extra money through vocational/technical [cooking, weaving] skills for female soldiers. For women to have a better capacity to do more things; these are always useful skills, in and outside of the KIO. Right now, there is no way for women to earn extra money so this is needed for women to earn an income."

Among other things, the overarching gendered division of labor results in positioning lower-ranking women as susceptible to becoming "minor-wives" (*num kaji*)[3] to male higher-ranking officers. While not unique to the military, this shows how rank intersects with gender to shape women's experiences of the army. This reservist comments that "it's kind of normal that the high-ranking officers have many affairs, other than their [wives]. You know, when they suddenly have a little more money than before they start thinking of how to have affairs with women." Another reservist I spoke to echoed these sentiments, saying that "for the women in the army, life does not seem so secure. One reason is that they are not leaders, so they cannot make the decisions, and another reason is that they get very low pay in the army. Some female soldiers, they get paid some money, and then go to stay with leaders or other men or like that. They are not allowed to make money outside [and men have their wives to support them?] so they try to make extra money like this. This is what I hear." Her colleague agreed, concluding: "If I could change one thing in the KIO, I would want to create more women programs, and help female soldiers earn extra money."

Exchanges such as these suggest that women's military participation is made possible through and within a war economy in which women are mostly recruited into lower-level back-office positions despite overarching changes to mobilization patterns that have occurred over the years. A rigid gendered division of labor, women's lack of prospects for promotion to command levels, and the absence of women in the Central Committee illustrate how rank collides with the political economy of gender in ways that create difference and distinction (Hyde 2024). Despite the hard work undertaken by female soldiers, the military standard is still the male body, making female soldiers impostors at best and deviant at worst. Herbert (1998, 21) reminds us that "the military is an 'institutionalized arena' in which the masculine is preferred over the feminine, and men are preferred over women. . . . It is one thing for women to enter occupations that were previously defined as 'male'; it is another to enter an occupation in which masculinity is so central a part of the definition of the occupation."

The myth of male military might, tied to combat, effectively writes over the experiences of women volunteering alongside men, fighting battles, tending to the wounded in stressful and harsh environments, and providing lifesaving material and physical support for little or no pay. It also distracts from the fervor of women like Nang Tawn, whom I met in early 2016, who told me that "since the conflict started, I've had this pull, that I need to join the army. I feel like I needed to join, to fight against the Burmese military. I feel like I am equal to any men in the military." Yet the perseverance of gender stereotypes depicting men as soldiers and women as the "beautiful souls" (Elshtain 1987) to be protected means that even women like Nang Tawn, who train alongside men with enthusiasm and dedication, are still seen as an anomaly to the armed forces.

As the experience of many women involved in this research shows, the gendering of the civilian-combatant distinction has served to obscure and devalue women's military labor. Yet they have participated in the war: both as formal soldiers and, as I explore throughout the book, as wives, mothers, and daughters providing much-needed militarized labor beyond the narrow category of "soldier." Therefore, the conflation of civilian status with women is based not on an assessment of what a person is actually doing during conflict and war but rather on an assumption stemming from gendered narratives depicting men as combatants and women as "peacemakers or as ancillary to conflict" as Trisko Darden (2023, 2) puts it.

The notion of women-as-civilians encourages the idea of women primarily contributing to military efforts outside the military organizations—as (potential or actual) wives and mothers. By barring women from continued military service upon motherhood and marriage, the KIO is able to more effectively benefit from women's household labor. At the same time, many women I spoke to, especially those who were recruited before the outbreak of war in 2011, admitted to wanting to leave the organization. They were just waiting for an opportunity to resign, valuing their life outside of the military. However, the KIO does not grant all leave requests easily, and women who are seen to have acquired skills of direct value to the organization are expected to stay. A member of the Central Committee explained that while "women leave the service after they get married, to give birth, to take care of their children . . . female members in the health or education departments, such as, teachers and nurses and doctors usually continue their work." When I asked why, he clarified: "Because it takes time to train those in medical and teaching, so the longer they stay the better." He added that they provide additional incentives for those who stay, even after marrying another soldier: "Sometimes they are married to military personnel, that means they get more support. Basic support from the organization, i.e., rice, cooking oil. For school teachers and health practitioners here, they might get, not a big house, but they do get housing support, so that they could continue to do their work and also receive support for both partners, so the conditions help them to continue their work." His statement suggests that a regular military salary is not enough to live on and hints at the idea that women are typically expected to provide the extra support needed for the family. The mobilization of women's military labor in education and health therefore means that the underlying conditions structuring women's labor remain in place. Such incentives confirm a broader division of labor, which locates (most) women as outside of the military organization despite military women's perseverance, dedication, and sacrifice.

Gendered Military Subjects

Extant research on rebel governance shows that rebel groups are to a large degree dependent on the communities living in their midst for information, shelter, and material support (Revkin 2021; Revkin and Ahram 2020; Stathis 2006). According to this body of work, women become key to revolutions when they can provide the group with "strategic and tactical advantages" (Asal and Jadoon 2020, 263), legitimizing armed struggles and incurring support (Wood and Thomas 2017). However, I have found that in Kachinland, the "advantages" that female soldiers bring are primarily material and affective rather than tactical or ideological: through their underwaged labor, female soldiers underpin the direct efforts of the war machinery, providing cheap but integral labor ensuring that frontline soldiers are fed and supported.

Thus, as shown by the experience of Seng Moon, recounted at the beginning of this chapter, women's labor and participation are critical to the survival of the Kachin resistance movement. Yet the traditionally feminine nature of much of women's work has served to naturalize it—and therefore to obscure and undervalue it (De Volo 2018, 66), exposing in particular lower-ranking women to experience discrimination and insecurity. However, inequality and injury exist in relation to military duty, pride, and commitment. As Hnin Wai (2024, 174) succinctly notes in her account of fighting in the Myanmar Spring Revolution: "When we women are treated as weak and pitiful creatures, even though we chose the same revolutionary path, we are forced to put in more effort."

The experiences of three women who joined the KIA in the early 1960s are illustrative of this: banded together by commitment and, I suspect, pure hard-nosed stubbornness, they navigated the obstacles they felt in their day-to-day lives by excelling in and not quitting the difficult military training. They distanced themselves from the broader efforts to position them as above all (weak and leaky) women rather than as military subjects as able as men to fight the Burman state: "The instructor scolded us in the training, when we were unable to catch up with the male soldiers: "You want to be a soldier, but you can't run up like the male friends." So we realized we have to try much harder than the male soldiers. We have to become better. And sometimes we managed to outrun the male soldiers. The trainers didn't like this, but what could they say." This has implications for the conflict: in the face of significant obstacles, women respond by becoming stronger, better, more dedicated soldiers, loyal to the national cause. But this new subject position also has implications for the next generation of women joining the military. By leaving existing gendered relations of power in place, young female soldiers are entering a masculine military domain in which the burdens of integration and adaptation are shouldered by women rather than by the military institution. Women are expected to use their feminine skills to complement male soldiers and, at the same time, manage prevalent stereotypes and stigma to gain respect. This is not an easy task. What this means for young women's everyday experiences of the military in the post-2011 cycle of the war will be explored in chapter 4.

AS TOUGH AS MEN
Women in the Military

"Why did you join the armed forces?" I asked a young private I met in Myitkyina in 2016. We were sitting in an old classroom, the midday heat in full bloom; a spider as large as my hand kept careful watch from its place on the wall opposite me. The young private played with a loose nail on her hand, sighed, and said: "I joined because my mum wanted me to. I mean, I also wanted to. I heard the news about recruitment on LaizaFM and so I joined." "Ok," I said, and nodded my head at her to go on. "What happened once you joined? Did you like your training?" She continued: "When we started the training, the teachers said that women just make [the army] weak: 'You are wasting your time here—women are not useful here,' they always said to us. But"—she emphasized—"I want to make things better for women in the army. I must work harder. I must pray."

Since the resumption of the conflict in 2011, the Kachin military has looked to women to fill its ranks in order to bolster its capacity. Yet, as this quote illustrates, women's participation in military activities upsets ideas about revolutionary masculinity, encroaching on the male privilege of military space. As a result, female soldiers may face both suspicion and discrimination, and their military careers are frequently curtailed by the idea that women should be homemakers, not fighters.

This is not a new phenomenon. As shown in the preceding chapters, women's responsibilities for ensuring militarized social reproduction as caretakers, homemakers, and mothers are framed as more important than their responsibilities as soldiers. Indeed, all of the (male) leaders I interviewed, whether they were currently in active service or had retired from it, repeated that women were too frail to be in combat and that their responsibility as mothers would in any case see them leave the army. As a high-ranking officer in the Eastern Division informed me: "We want more women to join and put their efforts into the struggle and to go into leadership. . . . [But] women want to get married and go home, so they cannot commit a long period of time to the KIO [Kachin Independence Organisation]."

Curiously, his view was not shared by the female soldiers I spoke to, almost all of whom understood marriage as an impediment to promotion. In fact, my interviews illustrate how young military women both recognize and attempt to upset this dominant gender order that sees women as mothers and wives first and soldiers second. Contrary to expectations, these constraints have at times resulted in strengthening rather than diminishing women's commitment to political violence: female soldiers navigate the insecurity they face by becoming even stronger, more committed soldiers.

This chapter foregrounds this contradiction at the heart of women's recruitment to the KIO and KIA (Kachin Independence Army) after the outbreak of fighting in 2011. In this period, women's labor has been both desperately needed and undervalued. Women, as much as men, are encouraged to join different training programs, such as the Education and Economic Development for Youth (EEDY) and the National Service (NS), in order to learn about and contribute to the activities and aims of the KIO/KIA, yet my interviews with military leaders reveal that men are preferred as active and actual soldiers.

As a (male) colonel puts it: "Because of the given circumstances right now, the military pressure is so strong and has intensified, so we need men to be trained faster and go to the frontline." At the same time, many families I met did not want to send their only son to war partly because it is harder for men to retire from armed service and partly because sons are expected to stay in the natal home after marriage. Sons also inherit land and property. After the resumption of the war, many of the young women I met living in liberated areas had therefore enlisted on behalf of their brothers, rendering female household conscription as a form of militarized social reproduction.

Female soldiers, especially the younger and more junior ones I met in Mai Ja Yang and Laiza, often claimed that they were more loyal and hardworking than their civilian sisters and expressed great pride and satisfaction in their work. Clearly, female soldiers were as (or more) dedicated to the national cause than male soldiers, but their military labor was often understood as a second, poorer choice, and suspicion was cast on women willingly living among men in the military. While this stigma did not determine the identity of female soldiers, it did shape the experience of many of the junior soldiers I met, who ended up spending much time and energy on contesting an overarching gender order locating them "as outsiders to the boys' club of the military" (Herbert 1998).

While chapter 3 focused on how a gendered division of labor structured women's inclusion in the military, this chapter seeks to understand what happened once women joined "the boys club": how did they experience the armed forces? In what ways did they respond to the gendered expectations and representations frequently accompanying female soldiers?

To answer these questions, this chapter traces the experiences of the many young, committed women who joined the KIO/KIA through EEDY, the NS, or regular household conscription after the outbreak of war in 2011. It tells the story of female soldiers negotiating—with much creativity, ambition, and strength—the restrictions they faced in the military. These strategies, ranging from rejecting marriage to advocating for a women's battalion and being "as tough as men," were not successful in removing gendered barriers and inequalities, even as they confronted dominant stereotypes and discrimination and emphasized Kachin women's abilities in the resistance efforts.

The women I met after 2011 believed in the purpose of the KIO/KIA to protect their community through military might and used their time with me to recount, often in detail, multiple generations of injustice and violence they and their families had faced at the hands of the Bamar state. However, their recruitment to the KIO/KIA did not erase this past discrimination, and at times, it even brought new insecurities. Women joining after 2011 were asked to contribute to resistance efforts in particularly gendered ways that did not upset but rather reaffirmed overarching gendered divisions of labor: men as head of household, army, and nation, women as their supporters.

Here it is important to note that no women I spoke to were drawn to the military for reasons of personal ambition or individual liberation; rather, all cited a sense of duty and responsibility toward their community. In fact, many of the female soldiers and graduates of the EEDY and NS programs I spoke to demonstrated a strong sense of empowerment by drawing on their dedication to the national cause and their capacity for endurance. "I want to be tough," one young woman I spoke to in 2017 told me. "I want to be a role model for our children so that they become more patriotic," her friend added. I found myself buoyed along by the optimism and dedication of the young female soldiers and officers I met, notwithstanding what I knew of the war: young women having to leave the armed forces early, straining to provide for what was left of their families, and having their military service viewed and honored as less of a sacrifice to the public than that of their brothers.

Education and Economic Development for Youth

Actually, among the youths, it has become a thing to become involved with the KIO! It's a good thing to be involved in their activities; your friends will look up to you.

—Civil society activist, Chiang Mai, 2015

The KIO is not just an army, they represent all of us Kachin. They support us socially and culturally. They give us education and teach us proper Kachin language. They are family.

—Civil society activist, Chiang Mai, 2015

The Education and Economic Development for Youth (EEDY) program provides students who have completed secondary school outside of KIO-controlled areas with a three-month-long intensive training in military tactics and practices. The program also includes courses focused on KIO/KIA history. The EEDY program ran for approximately thirteen years and, after a period of suspension, began again in 2017. Close to four thousand students graduated from the nineteen EEDY courses held between 2003 and 2015. Of these, 2,685 were men and 1,095 were women.[1] The aim of EEDY training is to increase support for the KIO's activities among Kachin youth living in cities, away from the rural areas under the control of the Kachin armed forces. For example, a high-ranking member of the KIO Central Committee (CC) explained that EEDY was established because "we [the KIO] learned that after so many years and decades of struggles our young Kachin in the city weren't speaking *Jinghpaw*, so we realized we needed to create a safe space for them where they can come and learn our cultural teachings and also understand about our revolution, the armed struggle."

Recruitment for the training is conducted via youth leaders in schools and churches and through youth groups active at universities throughout Myanmar. Once recruited for the training, students travel to training sites in KIO-controlled areas of Kachinland, where they are instructed in military tactics, political history, and Kachin cultural knowledge. Male and female students undergo the same training, wear the same uniforms, and carry the same heavy wooden rifles on their backs but live in separate barracks (Hedström 2016). When I first visited one of the training sites in 2013, I was met by an eager group of high school and university students who had journeyed from lowland Myanmar to Laiza. Clad in military green, they gathered around me to explain how excited they were to be attending the training. They showed me some of the things they had learned—how to salute the flag and hold a rifle—and thanked me for coming. They said they had made many new friends; some, I realized on later visits, had married after meeting each other through the course (as we will explore more in chapter 5). In other words, the course was not just hard work; it also appeared to foster a strong commitment to community and to the Kachin homeland through which revolutionary warfare was normalized. Older Kachins I met already understood the KIO to be a legitimate government; now the younger generation needed to be reminded about their duty and role in fulfilling the broader objectives of the Kachin nation. Young women could then be said to be socialized into the KIO "family" (as the quote at the beginning of this section intimates) where they would find new subject positions as active members of the KIO revolution. The program instills students with a sense of patriotic duty by disseminating the "ideological and political" vision of the armed forces, as the KIO puts it. It encourages the "military spirit," which will lead to "military action," as this older, now retired colonel explained to me: "The students are taught cooperation, management, leadership, these kinds of things. Most importantly, they learn about being tough . . . they have to have the military spirit and the military action. The military background will give you a stronger commitment, you know. I taught them what they needed to know beyond fighting, the ideological and political point of view, and about our vision and how to cooperate with other groups [in Myanmar]. . . . On the morning of the end of the course, they have a ceremony where they can show that they are ready to serve."

For each graduate I spoke to, the ceremony at the end of the course constituted the beginning rather than the end of their military commitment. Several people described it as a very emotional experience through which they reaffirmed a sense of connection to their Kachin homeland and to the army as the defenders of that homeland. All of the EEDY graduates I met described their experience in the program as critical for teaching them "the real history" of Kachin. They felt that their commitment to the KIO's political aims and objectives had been strengthened. The thoughts of a woman who had participated in the very first EEDY training held in 2003 are worth quoting at length, as they neatly illustrate three key themes that came through in most, if not all, of my interviews with female graduates—confidence, pride, and patriotism:

> The students who participated in the training, even [the ones who didn't want to attend], they feel very positive after the training about the KIO. . . . We become more patriotic. Most of all I think, for me, being patriotic means being more confident in yourself, being a Kachin woman. Before we didn't have a sense of this, we feel like being Kachin is not a good idea, we think that our Kachin accent, when we speak Burmese, is bad. We are trying to become Burmese, trying to speak with a perfect Burmese accent. So the training made people more confident, it taught us that being Kachin is nothing to feel shameful about.

The success of the EEDY initiative is also evident in the fact that, among my interviewees, the young Kachin women I met who had not participated in the military training uniformly expressed their desire to do so or, alternatively, their regret over not attending. This suggests that the rollout of the program has also contributed to an increased awareness about the KIO/KIA among people who have *not* attended. A young Kachin women's rights activist who attended the training while at university noted: "When I was in university, it was very famous. If you don't go to the EEDY you are not very popular, you know? [laughs]." What emerges from the experiences of participants is a picture of burgeoning nationalism framed within a military-administrative structure and a sense of comradeship and pride among the young people attending the EEDY program. This female interviewee, now working for a women's rights group, reflects:

> Before the training, I didn't really know about the KIO/KIA. What we see in the newspaper, we only see about the KIO/KIA being rebels, being bad people, things like that. When I read about them in the state newspaper, I didn't really know what they were fighting for. . . . I didn't really like doing the military training, but I liked listening to the politics, about the history of Kachin, the real history of Kachin, about where we come from and the names we held in previous times. . . . I think we were happy, there were many young people there and we made many new friends.

Graduates of EEDY training are listed as reserves rather than as active soldiers in the KIA, but to focus only on military membership is to miss how such practices are about creating subjects able and willing to labor for the revolution. Among the EEDY graduates whom I interviewed, a majority returned to their church activities or their universities at the end of the training. Some joined the KIO's women's wing, the Kachin Women's Association, or traveled abroad in order to take up positions with civil society groups focused on issues of relevance to Kachinland. This means that although none of the women interviewed joined the army upon graduation as soldiers, they were at the time of my interviews all working for causes in support of Kachin objectives, often in close cooperation with the KIO/KIA.

Much research on the ceasefire years, when the EEDY launched, focuses on the fact that the ceasefire agreements led to a period of much discontent among the general Kachin population, who were not well positioned to benefit from the agreements. The critical political ecologist Kevin Woods (2011), for example, notes that after the signing of the ceasefire in 1994, development projects across Kachinland ushered in a new era of "ceasefire capitalism," privileging local and national elites and overseas businessmen rather than local Kachin communities. The historian Mandy Sadan (2015, 247) suggests that activities undertaken by

Kachin diasporic networks and urban Kachin youths to protest against some of these activities led to a politicization of the Kachin community. Thus, after the outbreak of the conflict in 2011, "nationalist inspired groups of young Kachin people" quickly mobilized in support of the KIO/KIA. While I agree with the above analysis, I add that the expansion and success of EEDY training must be positioned as a key activity shaping support for the aims and objectives of the new leadership of the KIO/KIA. In other words, when the conflict reignited in 2011, an already politicized young public were easily mobilized and quick to state their support for the Kachin military cause. A substantial percentage of those were women, who had been socialized into the KIO family.

National Service

> All Kachins who are above 18 must enroll in the National Service (NS) programme for a two-year period regardless of their gender and educational background. [Only] married women can be exempted.
>
> —KIO CC member

The National Service program (NS) run by the KIO/KIA aims to increase actual conscription into the army by offering recruits the possibility of retiring after two years of service. This is a break from the old practices by which male soldiers (and female medics and teachers), once fully enlisted, could not leave until retirement. According to my interviewees, there was no formal retirement age, and people (especially men) could not easily leave. In order to leave the army formally, a soldier had to "submit [the] form for retirement, citing reasons like health, family and personal things that they need to take care of." Women, as already discussed, are typically asked to retire upon marriage.

The NS program represents a change from the prior focus on training reservists in the EEDY program, hoping to entice more people to join by offering them the possibility of retiring earlier than in the past. As a female reservist in the army told me when I spoke to her in Mai Ja Yang in 2017, "People are a rarity for the KIO." The fear is that the Kachin army will not be able to defend itself against the well-funded state military—by some accounts, one of the best-funded armed forces in Southeast Asia. As the quote from the CC member in the section above suggests, new recruitment initiatives have fostered a sense of unease, at least among some families I spoke to. The focus is on male recruits; in order to avoid conscription, people I met told me about families sending sons across the border to China or enrolling them in theological college. This leaves girls to be recruited. And as conscription is focused on the household, with each household

in KIO-liberated territories encouraged to support the army, young female soldiers I met often enlisted on behalf of their brothers, rendering female household
conscription a form of militarized social reproduction.

Indeed, among the female soldiers I interviewed who were at the time of
my interviews still working for the KIO/KIA, all but two had joined the army
through household conscription. When the call came to send a family member
to war, the daughters often enlisted at the urging of their families. A daughter
joining the army frees up time for male inhabitants of the household to engage in
other activities that may be deemed more valuable. This includes studying theol-
ogy in college or contributing to income-generating activities. This is illustrated
in the following quote from a young woman I interviewed. Although originally
from a KIO-liberated area, at the time of the interview, she was interning for a
Kachin women's organization in Thailand:

> In my village every family, every household is actively involved with the
> KIO. Every family has at least one soldier in the KIA. . . . But my father
> is a pastor and I only have one brother, and my parents don't want him
> to be a soldier . . . Our family understand that at least one person has to
> work for the Kachin people. We might not need to hold guns but can
> work for Kachin people in other ways. So I will work for the good of
> Kachin people and then my brother will not need to go. If he would be
> recruited in the future, my parents can speak to the local commander
> and make an exchange for me as I will work for the Kachin people.

An interview with the KIO/KIA confirmed that although they prefer male recruits,
if a household only has one son at home, they will recruit the daughter instead to
"accommodate family needs."

The practice of daughters enlisting on behalf of other family members renders
visible the importance of gendered intrahousehold bargaining[2] in the context of
war. A two-star medical officer I spoke to in March 2016 talked about her own
recruitment as a duty to both her family and the KIO. She explained that while
she has two brothers, they were both forcibly recruited by the state armed forces,
leaving her as "the only one who can do the duty." An interview undertaken with
a lieutenant who commenced working for the KIA in 1997 similarly drew attention to how a lack of bargaining power within the household pushed her into
army activities, explaining that as her brother had to take care of the family, she
was the only one able to sign up. "My brother was omitted from the draft because
he has to provide for the family," she explained. "So I volunteered for the family, on behalf of the family." The lieutenant later described herself as the "most
responsible" in her family; as the oldest sister and with only one brother, she took
it upon herself to join the army.

In this way, women's military duty cannot be divorced from their socially prescribed roles as "dutiful daughters" who in any case are destined to leave the household when they marry. Sons are supposed to stay in their family home. Together with their future wives, they will be responsible for taking care of their parents, property, and land, as a teacher at a KIO-affiliated school put it. "Someone has to look after the parents, and then the boy will stay and the girl will join instead of her brother." This is an aspect of Kachin culture the KIO understands might cause problems for their recruitment, and they try to resolve those problems by being reluctantly accepting in their responses: women who *insist* on joining, against the wishes of the military who prefers male recruits, are given access to the military. One colonel I met in 2018 said, with a sigh: "Yes, the generations depend on the male members . . . but our first choice for the army would [still] be for the man, but if the sister insists, says, 'No, I will go,' then we would take her." But what does this reluctance to accept female soldiers mean for the women who join the KIO/KIA?

Women Out of Place: Stigma in the Military

"Maybe women can also be seen as not so good after women spend a lot of time in the army with a lot of men," a woman told me with a shrug of her shoulders when I asked about how female soldiers were perceived in the community. Although the KIO has enjoyed a resurgence among the general public, concerns about army camps being morally corrupt spaces—at least for women—linger. In Western military contexts, this has been commonly analyzed in relation to gendered boundary work: because the military is a taken-for-granted masculine space where men are the soldier norm, female soldiers are defined by their gender and femininity, and stereotypes relating to women's perceived sexuality and availability abound (Herbert 1998; Pettersson, Persson, and Berggren 2008; Sjoberg 2014). This is a logic that helps differentiate the masculine soldiers from the feminized body/nation in need of protection (Elshtain 1987) and positions female soldiers as potentially disruptive, seductive, and dangerous. It is important to note here that the idea of women's bodies as seductive and tempting is reinforced by an overarching political economy that positions women as uniquely responsible for resourcing the armed forces. This logic both builds upon and reaffirms gendered narratives that associate women's bodies with motherhood, thus requiring the supervision and control of women's reproductive capacity. Moreover, when female soldiers are primarily positioned as potential mothers, they become above all female and, thus, out of place in the military.

As has been noted in other military contexts, when women are deployed to military missions, this runs counter to widespread societal expectations of women becoming mothers and running households. A study on female peace-keepers, for example, found that deployment for extended periods of time led to women being framed as too independent and tainted by their association with men and therefore, apparently, "unmarriageable" (Vermeij 2020, 3). Research on female soldiers in Israel has similarly noted how fears of "moral deterioration," in particular associated with women's presumed independence and closeness to men beyond parental supervision, emerged from (and therefore confirmed) broader gendered divisions of labor: women as mothers, and men as soldiers (Lomsky-Feder and Sasson-Levy 2015). These notions relating to gendered apti-tudes and roles are not in themselves harmful, but they expose female soldiers to discrimination and harm by undervaluing their labor and contribution to the broader military effort, distancing them from leadership opportunities, and emphasizing female soldiers' sexuality and reproductive potential.

The private quoted in the introduction said: "Some of our students, some of the boys, are touching us. They think that they can touch us and they think that women in the military, that we are very easy." She added after a pause: "After the training I was upset. But I prayed and prayed and found an answer . . . I decide to become a good leader so that I can represent other women, and do things for our nation."

A twenty-four-year-old nurse I met in Mai Ja Yang in 2016 told me that "they [the public] say that female soldiers are just a waste of time, that they get preg-nant, they gossip like that." A female nurse recalled how "once I was asked to help out at a wedding party [for a captain]. There I served food and drinks to civilians, and the civilians wouldn't speak to [female soldiers]." Soldiers, living far away from home, are not under the scrutiny of their families and are therefore susceptible to "corruption," especially female soldiers. The young private again: "I see many many bad things in there. . . . In our school, there were only five girls and 160 people in total. . . . Some of our leaders, they can choose which one they like in the military. The girls in the military, they are very far from the home and it's [a] difficult time and they are dependent on the men. And that's why they say that girls in the military are very bad and are doing bad things."

The stigma and suspicion that female soldiers face are related not only to their gender but also to the fact that they tend to be lower-ranking female soldiers from poorer communities. As discussed in chapter 3, there have been reports of inappropriate sexual relationships between lower-ranking female soldiers and higher-ranking male officers. During my interviews with soldiers, military train-ees, and women's rights activists, rumors and/or personal experiences regard-ing sexual harassment within the army came up frequently. A few interviewees explicitly referred to alcohol and sex as evidence of vices inherent in the army, which supposedly reflects badly on women but not on men. The private told me, with some annoyance, that "one guy said to me, if you want to get married, don't get involved in the military. If you are in the military, you cannot marry other guys because you will have a bad name." Recent data on harassment and gender-based violence experienced by cadets and soldiers within other national military organizations show that this remains a serious problem across countries, with female recruits often having to fight on two fronts: the actual enemy, and stereotyping and violence within the community, including within the armed forces (*Dagens Nyheter* 2017; Department of Defense 2023; MacKenzie, Gunaydin, and Chaudhuri 2020).

Although most women I spoke to conveyed a great sense of responsibility, pride, and duty in their work, many also expressed frustration regarding these gendered restrictions that had resulted in female soldiers having fewer opportunities for promotions, as well as the ways in which their strength and dedication were questioned by colleagues. The private quoted above explained how, during the military training, other male students would laugh at her and tell her that she should go home. She said: "The teachers also don't think that women should be involved in the conflict, and they can't accept the women's decisions." Many women directly linked these negative experiences to a lack of leadership possibilities for women. While the need for more soldiers has forced the army to more formally incorporate women in military activities, the increase of women on the ground has not been reflected either in the leadership or on the front line. Lower-ranking women seemed to be especially vulnerable to discrimination; the few senior women I interviewed did not voice many or any negative experiences.[3]

The private, like many of the female soldiers I spoke to, attributed their feelings or experiences of insecurity directly to the absence of women in leadership, explaining that the absence of women in decision-making positions made it difficult for them to openly challenge gender-based discrimination within the army. A reservist agreed: "When in the KIO, you are in a bubble, controlled by men you know." The lack of women in positions of authority means that female soldiers must navigate their circumstances within the context of a strict militarized and, above all, male hierarchy. The private quoted above explained that during the military training, she and the girls in the dorm "could not close our door. If we experienced problems, we could not tell the leadership because they are all men. We have to be patient ourselves and manage by ourselves, us five girls. We wanted to be able to close the door but they did not allow us to close the door. We slept very carefully."

These women's experiences touch upon different instances of gendered discrimination and violence, but read together, they refute the notion that these are

individual or occasional experiences. Instead, they reveal how structural problems and discrimination can, and often do, translate into experiences of direct
violence and harassment. However, in the face of this insecurity, female soldiers
navigate their positions in ways that underwrite both their own endurance and
survival as well as that of the armed forces. This means that women's military
labor is not undertaken simply in response to demands from above but is also
fueled by resistance, conviction, and nationalism. In fact, many female soldiers
I spoke to decided to respond to challenges by becoming even more committed
and hardworking soldiers—to be, in their own words, as tough as men.

Contestation and Persuasion: "As *Tough as Men*"

In 2013, I was visiting a training center for new recruits located close to the
China-Myanmar border. Over sweet drinks after an early lunch, slowly moving into the hottest time of the day, I began talking with Htoi Pan, a twenty-
three-year-old trainer who had recently joined the KIA. Around us, only the
chickens and some determined ants were moving; everyone and everything else
seemed to be taking a repose from the relentless midday sun beating down on
the red dust and green hills. Htoi Pan took her hat off and wiped her forehead.
I watched a procession of ants making their way across the rickety bamboo
table. For these new recruits, life is different from the older women who joined
in earlier cycles of the war. These younger women have access to the NS and,
importantly, the officer training school, which Htoi Pan had graduated from
and now taught for.

Htoi Pan told me proudly: "I want to give women the audacity to do more
things!" She continued:

> I want to contribute, even just a small, tiny contribution. That's why I
> do this: to contribute to the people, the Kachin people. My father used
> to be part of the people's militia. What I feel is significant. At the end of
> the training, there is a ceremony to swear the oath. There is a difference
> between swearing an oath and not doing this: you might be working for
> the people but it's not the same. Once you swear the oath, you become a
> real, full-time solider for the people. This makes a difference. This gave
> me a sense of duty.

However, women joining the military still construct and compete with militarized hierarchies of gender, negotiating their access to the military sphere
by becoming "as tough as men" and by differentiating themselves from civilian women. In doing so, they do not reject or erase dominant gender logics but

attempt to navigate around them. This is not a simple matter but a task demanding perseverance, persuasion, and contestation.

Although most of the women I met had been drafted, almost everyone expressed an eagerness to join and a clear wish to go to combat. As the determined young private quoted above put it: "We can't be selfish, we have to think about our nation, our Kachin people, our freedom." In fact, the majority of the younger (female) soldiers I interviewed argued that women should be able to go to the front line. They expressed readiness to sacrifice themselves for the Kachin cause, even though women are currently prevented from combat situations. Another young recruit told me: "In time of need, in time of severe fighting, I would be very enthusiastic to go. I sometimes think about going to the battleground but my officers worry about the security of women if we go to the frontline, so that's why we cannot go." Notably, all women emphasized the voluntary (and, thus, sacrificial) nature of their enlistment. No woman I interviewed told me that she was conscripted despite the fact that *all* of the currently active soldiers I interviewed had been conscripted, typically on behalf of their families. Rather, the soldiers I interviewed explained that they joined because they wanted to fight for the Kachin cause. The following quote, from a woman who entered the army just a couple of months before the conflict reignited in June 2011, now a second lieutenant, is illustrative of this sentiment: "I came to the KIA after I left high school. The reason I joined the KIA is because as a Kachin I have to serve, I have to struggle for our people. I was not drafted. I joined on behalf of my family as my brothers are very young and they need to go to school. Also, one of my younger brothers is in medical school, so I joined instead."

In referencing nationalism and duty to explain their current position, rather than conscription, they negotiated the gendered hierarchies that exist between civilian and military women. These suggest that military women are more dedicated to the Kachin cause and therefore worthy of more respect than civilian women. Specifically, the women created an alternative ideal for themselves as sacrificing soldiers, committed to Kachin military objectives. "I didn't inform my parents before I joined the army. I wanted to join because I want to be tough. It's tougher than being in the police. I really just want to participate in the military service to support the national struggle. . . . My family didn't mind. It's good because no one else has joined, so we needed a family member to join."

In situating themselves clearly within a framework of Kachin nationalism, female soldiers implied that regular civilians do not have the same commitment to the national cause and the Kachin nation as soldiers do. This is illustrated in the following quote from a medical corporal who joined the army in 2013: "Being a soldier means I am more solemn and serious, and feel more confident. I have an important role to fill, which is different from being a civilian. I am doing something important, and it is important how I behave and act. . . . I want my younger siblings to join the army too, when they grow up. The Burmese military and the Burmese state discriminate against us, so we can't be selfish, we have to think about our nation, our Kachin people, about our freedom." As this quote suggests, female soldiers are attempting to forge a new identity by highlighting their selflessness and their dedication to the national cause, clearly delineating themselves from civilian women. They do not openly oppose the stigma they experience but deploy a new identity as serious, sacrificing soldiers; the medical corporal quoted above even wants to sacrifice her younger siblings. Women's responses to the negative stereotyping they experience illustrate the limits as well as the possibilities of their position: they cannot openly challenge or change the perception of female soldiers as being "bad," but in our conversations, they created an interpersonal narrative about themselves that contested this construction. These narrative strategies are important because they reveal the possibilities available to the women as they negotiate the constraints of military life and the new subjectivities that arise from these gendered constraints. To contest or manage the stigma, lack of possibilities for promotion, and sexual harassment they endure requires the women to engage in difficult emotional and physical labor, showcasing both resilience and creativity. Here is the second lieutenant, quoted above, again: "Since I undertook the military training, I have gained a lot of confidence and I feel comfortable holding trainings and talking in front of people. . . . I would have liked to go to the frontline . . . but fortunately, by the grace of God, I was assigned here where I can train many good soldiers. Also, this is a very important job. . . . I have to be patient and work hard, so that I can train and promote many more brilliant soldiers."

Women employed other creative options to make the everyday, as well as the future, possible for themselves. About half of the currently active soldiers whom I interviewed were engaged in lobbying for a women's battalion and were carefully navigating the army's career ladder, which typically required a rejection of marriage. In their disavowal of marriage and insistence on combat duty, the women I spoke to both recognized and attempted to reject the dominant gender division of labor that positioned them as wives and mothers first, and soldiers second.

In fact, all of the soldiers I interviewed identified marriage as an impediment to their promotion. As this young corporal working in the third brigade put it: "I don't plan to get married anytime soon, as that means I must leave the army. We can't stay in the KIA with children." The second lieutenant, quoted above, agreed: "We usually joke with each other that we will only marry a military man so we can stay and have families in the military." Another officer, also a second lieutenant, explained that she and her female classmates "demanded the permission to let us go to the combat. We were just very excited to go. We wanted to go very strongly. We wanted to go to the battlefront." Instead, they were assigned office, logistics, nursing, and, more recently, city defense positions.

Driven by duty and patriotism, women's military service and, as we will see in chapter 5, their withdrawal from this, affords them a position from which they can contribute to revolutionary aims and objectives. At the same time, all of the interviews demonstrate the futile attempts by women to challenge the strict hierarchies of the military—revealing how gender ideals that are both nationalistic and militarized coalesce at the level of the individual female soldier, setting her apart from her male colleagues. In this way, despite the willingness of women to participate in the defense of the homeland—and the need for more boots on the ground—the KIO/KIA has traditionally restricted both the number of female soldiers and their assignment, often with reference to women's supposedly weaker and bleeding bodies (Hnin Wai 2024; Stern and Strand 2021). This is not an adequate explanation: indeed, as we have seen in the preceding chapters, women frequently perform backbreaking work and undertake hard physical labor, both within and outside the armed forces. Thus, while women's dedication and ability should not be questioned, their participation in armed activities is undoubtedly affected by their overwhelming responsibility for social reproduction. This, in the context of a prolonged conflict that has strained the coffers of the armed forces, determines not only the prevalence but also the experience of female soldiers in the Kachin armed forces.

While recent research has indicated the steep social costs rebel groups (may) incur by including women in their ranks (Wood 2019), the costs incurred by the female soldiers themselves are, and continue to be, steep. The anxieties sparked by women's intrusion into masculine/military space means that women who enter the military are by default "bad women": threatening to military cohesion and hierarchy (see Herbert 1998) and, by extension, threatening to the nation. Despite military women's strength, dedication, and creativity, assumed gender differences still mean that women's place within the resistance is primarily framed around their ability to reproduce the Kachin nation within the institution of marriage, to which we will turn next.

5

WEDDINGS AMID WAR

The Intimate and Insurgent Politics of Marriage

Shanglawt sumtsaw ga le
Kadai tsaw na mata

Freedom fighters' love spell
Who will be in love with it

College jawng num rai tim mung
High school jawng num rai tim mung

Hpaji n chye ai rai tim
Shang lawt myit sha rawng ra sai

Whether you are a college student
or a high school student
or uneducated
You only need to have the freedom fighter spirit

Wam dam ai tsaw e
Brang hpang de lawan wa rit

My wandering dear,
Come back to me quickly

Shang lawt hpyen jan tai ga
Battalian CO jan tai ga

Become the wife of freedom fighter
Become the wife of the battalion commander

Shanglawt Ration sha pyi jawm sha ga le
Ning nu hpe hkum tsun kau da
Mung lu jang she sen htu ga

Let's eat the freedom fighter's ration together
Don't tell your mother yet
Let's sign the marriage certificate when we got our country.

Na manang jang naw nga ai
Shi hpe mung saw sa wa rit

If you have yet a friend
Please invite her as well

"Shanglawt Sumtsaw" ("Freedom-Fighters' Lover")

—Composed by General Lahkang Pan Awng and performed by the band +3

The war has been a space not just for violence, fear, and trauma but also for love, duty, and affection. In the early summer of 2013, I was in Laiza interviewing female soldiers. A young woman from the local Kachin Women's Association (KWA) office named San Htoi had been assigned to help me organize these meetings, and each morning, she and her husband would knock on my hotel room door to pick me up.

Sitting in the car one morning, I asked the husband, Zau Ring, what he was doing and was told he was an active soldier. Zau Ring and San Htoi had met at an Education and Economic Development for Youth (EEDY) training organized two years prior. Although women and men lived in different quarters at the training grounds, they still participated in the same lectures and military exercises—and fell in love. They married after graduating, and nine months later, a baby boy was born. By the time of the baby's birth, Zau Ring had already been posted to the front line and San Htoi was working for the KWA in Laiza. The baby was with the maternal grandparents. When I arrived in Laiza, Zau Ring was home on permission for the first time since deployment. Scrolling through my phone for pictures of my rural home in Sweden over lunch one day, Zau Ring commented that it looked green and quiet. As quiet and peaceful as Kachinland will be one day, he added. The next morning, my last in Laiza, only San Htoi picked me up: Zau Ring had been called back to the front line. San Htoi was on her own again, the baby back with the maternal grandparents.

Many of the women I met in Laiza had experienced similar hardships to those of San Htoi and sympathized with her. They knew what life was like as a wife married to a soldier—almost always being left on their own after marriage, struggling for an income while providing for the husband on the front line and the babies back home—and cautioned their younger relatives not to marry a soldier or, as they put it, a servant to the Kachin Independence Organisation (KIO). Indeed, knowing this, almost all of the married women I spoke to told me they had not intended to marry within the army, but in the end, love or duty got the better of them. And as the popular song—"Shanglawt Sumtsaw" ("Freedom-Fighter's Lover")—recounted above suggests, loving the revolution means loving the soldiers. But what does it mean to love a soldier in the revolution?

Using oral histories from women married to male soldiers and interviews with officials performing weddings under the auspices of the KIO, this chapter attempts to answer that question by tracing the ways in which women make sense of and experience their intimate and political lives. It explores how officials within the KIO have attempted to shape marriage practices among the Kachin and considers how the intimate politics of marriage operate in the context of the changing dynamics of war. My interviews with women entering into relationships at different cycles of the war suggest that marriage is positioned as a critical resource for the KIO through which the organization generates affective, material, and political resources for the military, blending tradition and customs with military objectives. Women's labor in the household, as actual or potential mothers, is more important than their soldiering, as they are typically expected to leave the army upon marriage. To serve as a wife is to provide for the revolution, as married women help support individual soldiers and the army writ large through extensive, hard, and creative labor—yet the hardships experienced by women in providing for their families in situations of war and increasing poverty make married life all but impossible to sustain.

Similar to what Charlotte Al-Khalili (2023, 153–54) found in Syria, where, in the aftermath of the revolution, marriage ceremonies celebrated the merging of not just two families but two revolutionaries able to marry across sect and class lines, the war in Kachinland altered marriage practices. By lowering the dowry, enabling marriage across clan and kinship lines, and conferring legal identity through marriage certificates, the KIO has attempted to foster new armed loyalties geared toward the Kachin Independence Army (KIA) and a liberated Kachinland, helping to stretch the boundaries—and loyalties—of the household far beyond one's kin or geographical location. Feminist political economists have examined how social reproductive labor matters for state relations (Bhattacharya 2017; Elfenbein 2019; Federici 2012); here I build on these insights to argue that the everyday affective, intimate, and romantic relations sanctioned through marriage matter far beyond the individual household.

As a religious official affiliated with the KIO explains it: "The soldiers are getting old by serving in the military and most of them are away from their families and relatives. Therefore, it is very important and necessary to have the family of their own to support them so that they can be able to serve the military with enthusiasm and loyalty." However, marriage allows not only men to serve with "enthusiasm and loyalty" but also women who are positioned as political and legal subjects expected and able to contribute to revolutionary aims and objectives. In India, the anthropologist Alpha Shah (2013) has theorized relations of insurgent intimacy as crucial for understanding the social dynamics and mobilizing the reach of rebel organizations. In discussion of Karen National Union/Karen National Liberation Army's Brigade 5, Dominique Dillabough-Lefebvre (2025) has shown how close-knit networks of families and households are at the core of armed power, literally reproducing the Karen revolution (a seven-decade-long war fought between Karen nationalists and Bamar forces) through relations of insurgent kinship. I add to these discussions by focusing on the ways in which militarized marriage informs, indeed makes possible, revolutionary movements by helping to confer legal, material, and emotional benefits for the revolution.

Women's separation from their husbands and, sometimes, as with the case of San Htoi, from their children suggests that wartime marriages are not concerned simply with romance or love but are also a means for creating or controlling a gendered division of labor "in the service of the nation," as Sandya Hewamanne (2016) writes about war and postwar Sri Lanka (see also Baines 2014; Matfess 2024). In fashioning affective, legal, and material ties between soldiers and households, marriage provides stability for individual soldiers and confers legitimacy for the revolution writ large, which has allowed for the development of the Kachin revolution as a formidable armed and political force to be reckoned with.

Yet despite the KIO's attempt to engender "enthusiasm and loyalty" through marriages, the loyalties created through intimate relationships also produce tensions in the movement: women tired of the expectations put on them and their families request that their husbands retire from active duty or are stationed close to home, and warn other women off marrying KIO servants. What these experiences suggest is that women's labor has the possibility to reinforce as well as fragment intimate and military relations. Thus, although gendered inequalities are reaffirmed through an overarching division of labor that positions women—through marriages—as legal and political subjects in service of the nation, these roles are neither determined nor fixed: women do not necessarily become the kind of subjects that they are expected to be.

Military Marriages and Mass Weddings amid War

During the early years of the war, the KIA attempted to overhaul the ways marriages were organized,[1] including preventing excessive dowry payments made by
the husband's family to the wife's family (Sadan 2013, 336). Kachin communities
have traditionally been structured through a patrilineal kinship system wherein
"clan identity is traced through the male line, one does not marry into one's own
clan, and that exchange of women for marriage is one-way directed for each
instance of exchange" (Maran La Raw 2007, 56). This means that kinship structures are reproduced through weddings, and although these are neither impen-
etrable nor fixed, they nevertheless provide the foundation for Kachin national
identity and the current political struggle (Maran La Raw 2007). As the KIO
extended and solidified its reach after 1961, the military apparatus began to take
on social relations of authority, including intervening in these kinship-related
issues. As the historian Mandy Sadan reminds us, Kachin political leaders have
long been invested in fostering a united Kachin community (Robinne and Sadan
2007), and while their efforts to ban the dowry (N'Chyaw Tang n.d., 58) eventu-
ally proved unsuccessful, the practice of mass weddings and officers officiating
marriages between soldiers suggests that the intimate relations of everyday life
are, and have always been, instrumental to revolutionary aims and objectives.
Importantly, the issuing of marriage certificates creates subjects, materially and
politically, with duties toward and a place within a nation—Kachinland—framing the KIO as a legitimate actor on par with other states conferring legal identities and extracting loyalties.

As Srila Roy (2006) succinctly puts it in her analysis of the Maoist movement
in India: "In the case of both organizational and radical politics, the personal
is negotiated in contradictory ways—relegated, at times, outside the domain of
the political while constituting, at other times, the very object of a disciplinary
gaze." Within the KIO, marriage both embodies and illustrates a dynamic and
contested political construct: the modern Kachin nation as envisioned by the
KIO and contingent on the institution of marriage to foster new loyalties and
physically regenerate the nation.

The application of Wunpawng Mungdan—or Kachinland—to represent and
unite the various subgroups included under the Kachin umbrella thus also materialized in the organization of weddings by the KIO, as the KIO's official view is
that revolutionary marriages supersede ethnic differences. As discussed briefly
in the introduction, the KIO uses the term Kachin (or *Wunpawng*) to describe a
community of people belonging to six primary sub-groups. As Major N'Chyaw
Tang writes in his memoirs, the ethnic composition of this KIO-envisioned Wunpawng nation is "Jinghpaw, Maru [Lhaovo], La Shi [Lachik], Azi [Zaiwa], Lisu

and Ravang [Nung–Rawang]" (N'Chyaw Tang n.d., 58). This is not to say that
the kinship and lineage alliances underpinning this collective Kachin identity are
straightforward; on the contrary, political contestations about exactly who is to
be included under the broader Kachin umbrella have been (and continue to be)
controversial (Sadan and Maran 2022).

A member of the KIO wedding committee explained that "the KIO's policy is
reconciliation among Kachin [ethnic] subgroups [*amyu bawsang*]. So, we do not
reject or approve who they can marry or they cannot marry. This is all about their
personality and their right so we have no comment on their amyu bawsang." An
official with a Baptist church agreed: "When we organize the wedding individuals
or mass wedding, we do not pay attention to the subgroups. KIO is zero tolerance
on racial discrimination so the marriage would not classify on ethnic belonging."

The practice of mass weddings began in the 1980s, but they do not take place
on a regular basis. An official responsible for organizing weddings on behalf of
the KIO in Laiza said that since 2014, they have organized eight of these weddings in the headquarters,[2] where 213 couples have been married in mass ceremonies, paid for by the KIO and held either at a church venue or in a military
hall. A young woman who grew up in a liberated area explained to me that mass
weddings are a way for the KIO to show how much it values its soldiers, echoing
the sentiments of the officials interviewed for this book who stressed the importance of "enthusiasm and loyalty":

> The KIO organizes mass weddings, once or twice per year, for their
> soldiers. You know, everyone wants this kind of ceremony, even if big
> or small, so the KIO organizes like that to give encouragement to sol-
> diers and to provide for the soldiers. The soldiers don't have money or a
> salary, and don't have holidays so how can you do a wedding like that?
> Everyone values a wedding, and the KIO values its soldiers so it orga-
> nizes the weddings for them. In our culture, if you don't have a proper
> wedding, people view you badly. So in order for the soldiers to be equal
> and happy in the community, it's important for the soldiers to be mar-
> ried. If you don't have a proper wedding, you don't feel good inside.

The mass weddings are ambitious as well as arduous events, carefully planned in
detail by a committee made up of officials from different departments within the
KIO, including the Central Committee, responsible for managing the weddings
and the steps leading up to them. Before a couple can get married, interested
individual soldiers must submit a wedding leave permission to their higher-
ranking officer. This can only be done if the soldier has served for at least five
years (in the case of men) or three (in the case of women), and indicated interest

in participating in the mass wedding. The KIO then collects and reviews the list of couples in the area ready to be wed and interviews all of the couples. After that is done, the KIO's "wedding committee" reaches out to the relevant pastors or priests to set the wedding date and wedding rehearsal dates as well as three days of Bible practice. They also take measurements for and order traditional wedding clothes (different for different subgroups), the wedding rings, procure the Kachin sword, and produce the marriage certificate. As one official remarked with a sigh: "It is not an easy job to organize the mass-wedding. We have to manage all details, like taking the right wedding ring size from the brides and remember the couple's names for the wedding certificates." After the wedding, the new wife—if a servant of the KIO—is usually allowed to leave the military, suggesting that for the KIO, women's labor in the household holds more importance than their work as soldiers: women's duties are in reproducing the revolution through careful reproductive and productive labor, including childbirth and the fashioning of new legal and political subjects with loyalties toward the KIO.

Another important actor is the Kachin Culture and Literature Committee, which is not under the KIO but an association initially set up in the early 1960s by Jinghpaw-speaking nationalistic students to promote and protect, as the anthropologist Ying Diao (2021, 673; my emphasis) puts it: "*one* official Kachin history and culture." Some of these students were part of an underground movement called the Seven Stars, which later formed the KIO (Sadan 2013, 250) as recalled in the introduction to this book. The Kachin Culture and Literature Committee is responsible for "doing the culture thing," as many of my interlocutors phrased it: gaining permission from the families for the wedding and agreeing on the dowry. As noted above, the dowry—alongside the old system of chiefs—was officially rejected by the KIO in 1969, with General Secretary Zau Sen leading by example by marrying his wife without any dowries being exchanged (N'Chyaw Tang n.d., 58). Yet the dowry has proven difficult to abolish, with young men and women I met as late as 2018 telling me they would not want to get married without the exchange of a significant dowry. After the outbreak of war in 2011, religious, political, and military leaders came together to, again, discuss the dowry, announcing that it should be a maximum of 300 USD across Kachinland. "Weddings are huge and expensive, and that's why people don't get married," a woman working in civil society told me before she revealed that neither her nor her friends would marry without a substantial exchange of dowry: it would be embarrassing to do so. She explained: "Even my friend's father, who was at the meeting deciding on lowering the dowry, said he didn't want his daughter to get married cheaply."

However, in the armed forces, the dowry is often adjusted down (if asked for at all), as the soldiers do not have enough of an income to pay a substantial dowry. "Since they are serving at the military," a pastor told us, "most of the brides' families are not asking for a high rate of dowry. They are already aware that the soldiers are serving in the military and not making money." Reflecting on her dowry, a woman married to a soldier similarly explained: "When we married, it was too difficult for my family and relatives to travel to KIO controlled areas. And I didn't want to burden them simply because I and my husband were serving at KIO. My parents really understood this and they happily allow me to marry with a servant of the KIO and they did not request the dowry fee so much. My father even lowered the dowry."

Marriage is important both for the organization as well as for the individuals who do not want to just cohabit (which, as noted above, is looked down upon) yet have not been able to afford a wedding or receive leave from their superiors to hold a wedding. "Some couples do not have money to hold the ceremony but already got two or three kids," a pastor working in the KIO headquarters said. "According to religious beliefs, children born out of wedlock are lacking the blessing and also it is not good for the KIO image as well. So that's why we the KIO organize the mass wedding for the couples and households who are not married yet." It is also important in terms of regenerating the community and strengthening ties to the KIO.

Marriage, which is strictly heterosexual, functions as a way for the organization to engender material and affective support for soldiers and the army writ large. The pastor again: "The marriage is important to our Kachin people since our population is still very low. It is kind of promoting our culture by bonding two families together and growing the population rate. And it also [is] very important to the KIO as well." Marriage is here situated as critical for physically regenerating the supposedly dwindling Kachin population and sends a message of coherence and stability, arguably all the more important during times of violence and war.

As such reasoning reveals, households in which the institution of marriage is physically and symbolically materialized are recognized as central to the revolution by the KIO. Wives provide stability as well as emotional and material support for male soldiers who sometimes are away for years on end without regular financial or material support from the army. One young woman I spoke to recalled that she did not see her father for more than five years: her parents were married in the late 1970s, and as the war intensified, men were called away to fight. When she finally met her father again, she did not recognize him. This was not an isolated experience; during times of war, soldiers in the KIO primarily serve the armed forces rather than their immediate families, with especially low-ranking soldiers stationed away from home for months or even years on end. Thus, in the lived experience of marriage, to be physically together does not seem to matter as much as the affective and emotional ties that are forged between wife and soldier and the political and legal ties generated between the household and the KIO. These ties animate the revolutionary cause, providing much-needed material and spiritual sustenance.

Married to the Cause: Experiences of Married Life within the KIO

Most of the soldiers' wives that I spoke to in the course of my research had met their husbands through the military. Some recently married couples like San Htoi and Zau Ring met and fell in love at the EEDY training facility, whereas others had been introduced via friends in the military. Despite feelings of love, most women I met had not wanted to marry a soldier because they knew his loyalty would always be to the army first and foremost: a soldier is a servant, they would explain time and again. Moreover, a soldier's pay is bad, if it comes at all, and positive experiences are often reliant on having good relationships with higher officers who are able to grant leave requests, provide extra money for housing or sick family members, or support the costs of proper weddings. Women know that life married to a KIO servant will be anything but easy, as Htoi Bu recalls in the next section, with women expected to shoulder the brunt of the burden for maintaining both household and military life.

In other words, it is not so much that wives are called to "eat the freedom fighter's ration" together with their husbands or boyfriends, as the popular song above claims, but rather that they pay for, prepare, and provide the ration for the soldiers as well as for themselves, their children, and extended family. As Emma Dowling (2016) powerfully writes: "Love does not come for free and indeed costs some people more." Women are often expected to work harder, perform more, and receive less in the political economy of intimacy, yet this is also work that is obscured by military elites and in the stories we tell about war in which men are protagonists and heroes, rather than the women whose labor makes all of their achievements possible.

While ostensibly honoring and recognizing the labor of women, these revolutionary marriages reaffirm a gendered division of labor that can be utilized for the broader interest of the revolution. Yet women's work has remained largely invisible. To reveal the importance and impact of women's reproductive work on both the war and on the women themselves, I next highlight three women's marriage stories, each married in different cycles of the war. While these women are not necessarily representative of all women married to soldiers, their stories do reveal how marriages are lived within the context of the war and, importantly, how women are positioned—as legal or political subjects—within them. This helps to explore how and in what ways marriage relates to the Kachin political project and foregrounds women as key political actors in nation-making projects.

Htoi Bu. Married during the height of the conflict in the 1980s. Has two sons and five daughters. Is a former female soldier.

Marriage life journey with a KIA soldier was not easy. I joined the military in 1974 and I served about eight years. I met my husband there. He got a crush on me on his first sight and his friends also told him that I might be a good housewife. My husband liked me so much and proposed to me but I didn't reply because I felt that I was not old enough to get boyfriend. He sent many love letters but I did not respond to him because I had made the decision that I would not marry in the military. He also asked his senior's help to get us married. I felt so annoyed and finally said yes. Even though we became boyfriend and girlfriend, we both were serving at the military and had our duty in different places.

When we finally got married, we did not have a chance to do any culture-related things. His family was away and I was also away from my family. And the situation that time was, we could not easily communicate or access to our families as we served in the military. But we got help from our higher-ranking officials who gave us kitchen supplies and furniture. Two weeks after we got married, my husband left for his duty. As for me, I applied for my discharge order, which I got once I explained that I had to take care of my mother-in-law.

Once I got my discharge order I moved around to sell any kind of goods. But when my pregnancy was reaching eight months I just stayed and sold things at my place. And I learn sewing as well. To increase our family income, I decided to sell and sew at the same time. My husband was busy with his army duties so I had to take every household responsibility like as housekeeping, babysitting, income generating so on. Since my husband could not earn any income, I had to support everything he needed, such as cigarettes, food, soap, toothpaste and so on. I do not know how to express in detail that what kind of support I provided him with. It was really stressful when my kids got sick because there were no other hands for taking care of my kids and earning money.

For the dowry, we arranged this when the situation got better. His grandfather went to my home to do the culture thing. My brother gave him a sword and blessing for our marriage life. In 1998 we finally paid dowry about 20 lakhs. The dowry might be small but we assisted as much as we could to my family. We got a marriage certificate from church, and not from the Department of General Administrations, which issued these before the ceasefire in 1994. But after the ceasefire church officials could travel to KIO-controlled areas, so they could take over this responsibility.

Since my husband was away, I faced many challenges and hardships in raising my kids and earning money for their education and our survival. So finally, I went to the KIO chief and requested my husband back. He came home, but then the political tension began and in 2009 he was not granted sick leave even though he was very unwell, because we had a very fragile political situation. He died. I can't express how difficult of my marriage life has been.

Seng Gu. Got married during the ceasefire years. Works as a cook. Has four children.

He was my second husband and I was his second wife. He was recruited in the KIA army in 1975. After ten years of service, he got his Discharged Order due to a health condition, and became a car mechanic. I lived with my sister's family doing gold mining. He asked my sister for permission to marry me. We just did a small culture thing, instead of a wedding so we did not get a marriage certificate until we moved to Laiza.

When we started our life journey together, we faced many difficulties. At first we lived in his hometown. Most of the money that we earned we had to send to his parents. I was very busy with house works and taking care of my mother-in-law, who lost her vision, and also ten of my husband's siblings' kids during my second pregnancy.

We came to Laiza to earn money. When we arrived in Laiza, the quarter leader asked me about my husband's military personal number and his discharge order number in order to assess if he was a veteran or if he had left the army without permission. I replied that I didn't know his details because the KIO was tightly restricted in government-control areas, even for the veterans, so he had not kept all the documents. They noted him down as a veteran. Later, I think in 2009, when the political tensions increased, the KIO organized the Local Defense Force which he joined.

Life in Laiza was full of challenges. My husband was posted to the Local Defense Forces so I had to work hard. I worked as a daily worker for cutting and clearing the farmyard. I worked six days a week. I got up early and prepared for my elder kids to go to school. I made a rice soup mixing with milk powder for my breastfeeding baby and I left him with one of my neighbors. I earned 1,500 kyat per day but I had to pay 1,000 kyat to the babysitter. I did not miss any chance of day job opportunity which came up, I just took it. Every time I went for a day job, I left my breastfeeding baby with the babysitter. And I also made military uniforms. I worked any kind of job because I needed to feed my kids. I also served as much as I could at the church as cooking, cleaning and decorating. I was assigned as a deputy head of women department of our quarter's congregation parish. I also was appointed by the KWA as a secretary of our quarter. At the same time, I also raised ten pigs as well. But when the war resumed in KIO control areas, I had to stop farming, due to security reason. I even can't express how my marriage life was so difficult.

Due to family hardships, my husband had requested many times to resign but there was no one replace him. But when our son signed up for service, my husband was able to resign after ten years. But then he passed away with tetanus.

Cecilia. Worked for the KIO administration. Got married during the new war. Has three children.

After I took my high school exam in 2009, I went to Laiza to earn an income. I was working at [a] local administration office as a clerk. While I was working at there, together with some friends and colleagues I applied for KIO membership. After one month, six of my friends were sent to take military training, but me and my other friend were transferred to the municipal court for our service. That time, my now-husband was working at the administrative department office. At their department, the number of staffs had increased a lot, so their barrack was crowed, which meant that he had to be moved to the compound I stayed at for my service. So that's how [we] met, and fell in love and became a couple. In 2010 he came to my house for the engagement. He was from the brigade area so none of his family member was able to accompany him; it was just him, and he could only pay 3 lakhs in dowry. My parents did understand that he was a KIO servant and could not pay more for dowry. We began living together and then I got three months pregnant.

My husband didn't want me to be a soldier so he didn't let me take the military training. When my senior clerk heard about my engagement, he told my husband that I should have got discharge order before I got married. So I came back to Laiza and applied for the discharge order.

Due to the political situation, which was very unstable, he had to go back to his barrack as soon as possible and we could not negotiate about our wedding ceremony. I stayed with my parents and he went back to Laiza, to serve. I gave birth to our first daughter in 2010, and we finally got married when she turned three. He received a month for wedding leave, but then he went back to his barracks and I continued to stay with my parents, as he had no place for his family in Laiza.

He could not support to us because the monthly stipend for a KIO servant was only 10,000 kyats, and he didn't even get his stipend monthly. He received it mostly bi-annually. He got neither paternity leave nor financial support. In fact, we didn't receive any support from the KIO.

When my second daughter had to [be] sent to the nursery school, we needed more money, so I had to find a job. By the end of May 2018, I got a job as a cashier. After I got this job, I could support my family a lot, and especially when he went for short course trainings.

I have heard that receiving supports for lower-ranking soldiers is dependent on their higher officials. My husband reported to his higher officials about the hardship of family being apart and he requested a space for me and our kids to stay in Laiza. Finally, his officials agreed to give a space for our family and we were able to reunite in 2017, seven years after we got engaged and four years since our wedding. I got my third daughter in August 2021.

The Social Contract of Marriage within the Armed Forces

Marriage helps realize the KIO's revolutionary objectives, beyond the conferring of legal and political identities. For Htoi Bu, Seng Gu, and Cecilia, their marriages to KIA soldiers pushed them into a chapter of even harder work, as the labor involved in ensuring that they and their families were surviving in the midst of war has been as extensive as exhaustive. As discussed in the other chapters of this book, women married within the KIO become responsible for keeping households and individual soldiers fed and clothed, and the types of militarized social reproduction they engage in demonstrate both creativity and perseverance, as this quote by a woman who got married in 2011 against her family's wishes illustrates:

> After we married, my husband spent most of his time in the military even though he was just with the volunteer force. So, I have had to take responsibility for earning an income. I leave my kids with my neighbors and take day jobs. It is really not easy to be a wife of KIA soldier. But I'm not afraid of anything and I can work hard. Our family cannot rely on him, even when he was a volunteer soldier. I already know that he would be busier than before, since he became a permanent soldier with the current political situation. I'm not afraid at all since I have strength to work hard and I can take care of my family.

As with Htoi Bu, Seng Gu, and Cecilia, militarized social reproduction here includes juggling a variety of chores ranging from basic subsistence farming to raising animals, sewing uniforms, nursing children back to health, and sending all sorts of support to the front line. Reflecting on her "marriage journey," another woman interviewed for this book explained that being married to a KIO servant means that women have to take "every household responsibility." When asked what this entails, she elaborated on a long list of the different duties, which stretched beyond the physical boundaries of the household—from housekeeping to income-generating activities. She added that they also have to provide for the front line. As she recollects it, lower-ranking KIO staff members did not receive a regular stipend, leaving her to support her husband "with everything he needed." This apparently included but was not limited to clothes, cigarettes, food, soap, and toothbrushes. She concluded: "I do not even know how to express in detail that what kinds of support I provide him." Taken together, these women's experiences illustrate how women's labor extends beyond the immediacy of the home, as households include husbands posted as soldiers and children looked after by grandparents, with wives being at the core of the household. As their stories show, told with pride as well as exhaustion, women's work animates as well as maintains webs of relations spanning the households and the armed forces. This, importantly, helps to reinforce the collective project of Kachin survival and indicates how marriage helps to situate women as subjects in relation to and with responsibilities toward Kachin military authorities.

To understand the ways in which the intimate politics of marriage operate in the context of the changing dynamics of war means to recognize that intimate lives are enmeshed in military structures. My analysis shows how women's intimate labor goes far beyond the household to reproduce and realize a Kachin nation as envisioned by the KIO. In villages across Kachinland, these intimate relations serve to materially and emotionally sustain the armed revolution while emphasizing the role of individual households within it. The centrality of militarized social reproduction to revolutionary goals and objectives, here understood as the intimate and emotional labor performed by women through the institution of marriage, is clearly recognized by the KIO, demonstrating how the Kachin revolution cannot be understood without consideration of the gendered aspect of civil-military relations. The organization of weddings and issuing of marriage certificates reproduce the revolution in both material and ideological ways by creating new legal and political subjects with loyalties and responsibilities toward Kachin authorities. As scholars of legal identity have noted, to be recognized as a state, nonstate armed groups like the KIO must produce citizens to govern, (Fortin, Klem, and Sosnowski 2021) and, I would add, to generate resources from. Thus, in the intermeshing of military, religious, and customary traditions, the marriages arranged under the auspices of the KIO fuse clans with military customs and legal responsibility, helping to support the KIO and its ambition for an autonomous Wunpawng Mungdan.

Many of the women I met told me they wanted this too—a liberated and free Kachinland—but none wanted to marry a soldier. Citing hardships and poverty, older women warned younger women off marrying within the KIO. Indeed, as the stories included in this chapter show, young women's marriage journeys, facilitated by the KIO, reaffirmed a gendered division of labor and the military's reliance on the household for sustenance and support.

Writing of Hugo Chávez's Bolivarian revolution, Rachel Elfenbein (2019) has emphasized the importance of women's unpaid labor, maternal roles, and women's organizing for enabling Chávez's political vision. In Kachinland, women's labor, as realized through the institution of marriage, has similarly facilitated Kachin revolutionary goals while deepening a gendered division of labor. At the same time, women have also leveraged these positions to push back against KIO demands, asserting claims—to their husbands or to financial support—and showing pride in their work and their contribution to the revolution. Yet so much of this labor, essential for community survival as well as state recognition, remains invisible.

Conclusion

RELATIONAL LABOR AND REVOLUTIONARY FUTURES

In 2023, I undertook final interviews with women living in displacement camps. The women, all mothers, had been living in displacement for more than ten years. Their children grew up in the camps, and the women have had to learn how to cope with scarcity and insecurity. One woman, a mother of two, tells me: "Since I was forced to flee from my original home, I have never been happy. Not for a single day." She is quiet for a while and then adds: "Maybe I was a little bit happy before the coup, sometimes. But after the coup, the situation is worse."

The military coup in 2021, a violent and brutal event that galvanized countrywide protests and elicited even more violent and brutal responses by the military regime, has also been felt in the northernmost border of Myanmar, in areas under the control of the Kachin Independence Organisation and the Kachin Independence Army (KIO/KIA). However, in some ways, the coup is just the latest episode in a long history of war and violence in Kachinland, where women's labor upholds community and kin. In this book, I have shown how women's labor is shaped in relation to the broader political economy of war and, therefore, how it changes in relation to different cycles of war. During periods of increased violence, when the very relations underpinning community life are targeted in counterinsurgency campaigns and access to lands, farms, and markets is cut off, women's labor becomes even more urgent: they raise pigs and chickens, find work on farms or in casinos, make up the shortfall of manpower in the armed forces, and marry soldiers in revolutionary weddings. As this illustrates, militarized social reproduction is more than mere subsistence; it is labor shaping collective identities and forging ties across generational and geographical divides.

Crucially, this labor also changes in relation to women's life stages, reflecting how the work of sustaining life in times of crisis and war is an ongoing, dynamic, and, at times, almost impossible practice.

In this final chapter, I reflect on how the cycle of violence, post-coup, has affected women in Kachinland and their capacity for militarized social reproduction. I examine how women's labor, articulated and produced at different levels and contexts—from the intimate politics of everyday life to community labor undertaken within displacement camps and army brigades—enables revolutionary life to be lived, not only in the present but also in the future. I trace the effects of this labor on the women engaged in it, in the forms of depletion and dedication, pride and exhaustion. I show how love, care, and affection are what enable families and soldiers to endure war and sustain revolutionary objectives.

In centering on mundane, everyday practices, rather than spectacular stories of strategic wins, heroic actions, or violent deaths, I demonstrate how women's labor is, in fact, nothing short of spectacular. Women's labor is what gives the revolution its forward momentum across cycles of war.

Militarized Social Reproduction after the Coup: "I feel like a widow even though my husband is still alive"

"Until the coup," a woman in her fifties tells me, "I had a good struggle. Of course, we live in displacement, but we had some happiness, my husband and I. We struggled together." Her husband is a soldier, but up until the military coup, he was able to take leave when his family needed him. She explains: "I was mostly on my own but he came home when he was needed. He helped build our chicken coop and the pigsty, for example." Now she fears they might not see each other again. He cannot come home, she says, and she cannot go out and work as a daily laborer. They have almost no income, but still, she has to support her family as well as her husband on the front line. She says: "Before the coup I didn't have to send him things for his personal use. But now, I have to buy things like medicine, soap, and cigarettes for him."

Another woman agrees, saying: "Before the coup, my husband could come home, but now he is needed at his post 24/7, and I now also have to support his necessities." She explains that before the coup they would get by on his salary and her work; even though he was not paid every month, getting a lump sum of (overdue) payment was actually preferred, as they then could use that for a down payment on animals, which they now might have to sell to survive. "After the coup," a married woman with one child explains, "I feel like a widow! I never see my husband but I still have to provide things for him, like raincoat, shoes and cigarettes." She adds: "I understand that their duty is to protect our people and our lands, so I don't want to bother him, and I don't want to give any stress, but now I feel depressed. I just want my family back."

As I have argued throughout this book, the burden of militarized social reproduction is heavier in communities affected by conflict and must be understood to be a direct consequence of the war, with women displaced from their communities, living in fractured households, and removed from arable land and markets (Johnston and Lingham 2020). Importantly, living and working in displacement produce a form of militarized social reproduction that extends beyond the individual household: it here becomes a collective reproduction of the community through everyday as well as exceptional acts of labor and duty that do not only support soldiers and families materially but also renew and reproduce the nation. The women we have met in this book often worked collectively; with displacement, their village and family units were torn apart, and people were dispossessed not just from their lands but from their kin too. Due to the sheer number of women and the absence of able-bodied men, women would labor together in groups, joined by physical proximity and ethnic identity. Members of a local civil society organization I met in Laiza commented that "most [displaced] women's husbands serve in the KIA, so women are heads of households and have to take more responsibility now. In the village, women are helping each other, so their mindset is that they look out for everyone, the whole village." As Ina Zharkevich (2019, 149), writing about the Maoist conflict in Nepal, argues: "In times of war, the boundaries of one's kin stretch far beyond one's natal family."

In displacement camps and in army brigades, watching women interact with each other and the people around them illustrated to me how women's labor took place in open kitchens and in homes lacking doors, yielding households bounded not so much by walls as by the community. In this setting, women's labor takes on a particular urgency, underpinning the social relationships that produce not only the new home but also the extended nation. Through militarized social reproduction, the relationships among the home, the army, and the nation are renewed daily, allowing for the evolution and sustainment of the Kachin revolution. Soldiers, former and current, would step in and out of the household unit, with children playing in the bunkers dug out of the red earth surrounding the houses. Occasionally, one of the women would stop her work to joke with a visitor, almost always a soldier, underscoring how this labor takes on meaning within, not outside of, military relations and conflict.

Importantly, the material and affective ties forged through women's labor underpin the social relationships that produce not only the home but also the extended nation, even when this work is undertaken *outside* of the nation: a wife of one of the injured men I interviewed in chapter 1 reportedly also worked in China at a casino. Thus, this is labor that is, above all, relational, shaped not only in reaction to shifts in the broader conflict economy but also to collective identities and relationships that are sustained through women's everyday practices.

Especially within communities torn from these women's homes and lands, the importance of marriages and household relations for forging community relations and ethnic boundaries become particularly acute. Women's efforts to "make meaningful life" (Faxon 2020), then, do not matter just for their capacity to repair and nourish relationships and bodies but also for their capacity to forge new ties to the home and the armed forces. One older woman I spoke to, one of the first members of the Kachin Women's Association, recalled how in the medical center she and the other wives ran for injured soldiers, marriages would frequently have to be arranged among the soldiers, the female nurses, and the cooks who helped out. "They fell in love with the women," she said, "and so we had to help with the weddings." Intimate relationships and ties, and the kinds of gendered relations of labor they emerged from, are essential for understanding the sustainment of the Kachin nation, with marriage in particular constituting a key resource that both underpins the revolution and provides women with a platform to inform the wider dynamics of the war, as we saw in chapter 5.

However, it is worth remembering that women's labor and support are also cheap and therefore affordable for a small armed group engaged in revolutionary warfare. A women's camp committee member working in Je Yang camp, the largest in Kachinland, remarked that "although women's groups work so hard and have greatly contributed not only to the whole community, but also to the revolutionary cause, by cooking for soldiers in the frontlines, nobody has given them even a Yuan." She added that "many women feel discouraged and complain a lot, but we encourage them, and try to convince them that they are doing their duty for the cause of the Kachin nation." As we have seen in this book (chapters 1–3), an overarching gendered division of labor has resulted in obscuring both the value of women's work for the broader war effort as well as the importance of their sacrifices.

These women's experiences of depletion and depression reflect a long durée of discrimination and violence. This is illustrated in seemingly benign processes of budgeting and investment. For example, the prioritization of military expenditures by the central government has meant that a large proportion of the population has had to rely on informal coping mechanisms to care for the ill, the elderly, and the very young. According to the World Bank, right before the coup, the Myanmar government spent around 3.6 percent of the total government budget on health care. Although this represented a slight increase in budget spending on welfare,[1] this number was still low—especially when compared to what has been spent on military infrastructure, which was notably higher (and, after the military coup, rising).[2] Indeed, after the coup, when the State Administration Council (SAC) took power from the elected government, SAC increased defense spending while at the same time significantly reducing spending on education, health, and welfare.[3] As this book has documented, in the absence of a formal social safety net, women have taken on additional responsibilities to ensure the welfare of their near and extended families. Nowhere is this need more acute than in conflict-affected areas of the country where the destruction of health infrastructure and the politicization of humanitarian aid by the central regime, alongside the very real impact of war on people's physical security and mental well-being, have resulted in large proportions of the population wanting for basic health care and other services. In internally displaced persons camps around Kachinland, the deteriorating security situation together with the blocking of humanitarian aid by the SAC cause families and households increased stress and trauma. Women I speak to fear they will never be able to return home again. They fear for their husbands and children. They fear jets attacking them. One woman told me: "I need this war to end so that my family can be together again." She added: "But I cannot just give up."

These intimate relations of everyday life—where women are toiling to make ends meet—is where the war is acutely felt and experienced. Amid the disruptions caused by the war, women's labor is what enables life to be lived, not just in the present moment but for the future too.

A woman who fled to a camp in 2011 shares: "Yes, after the coup my life is more difficult even though it hasn't changed all that much." She continues:

> I have had to cope with the fighting and the war all my life, since I was a child. The SPDC [State Peace and Development Council] would come to my place and burn down my village. I would have to move again and again, since I was ten. At that time, [government troops] arrested everyone in my village and forced us to live in a military camp. They burned my village down. My father was tortured to death. When you asked which time was better, since my childhood everything has been bad. The only difference in my life now and before the coup, is that before we had more humanitarian aid, and now we do not even have that.

She feels a lot of stress and anxiety. Before the coup, she and her husband would both go out for daily labor and get some humanitarian aid. Now they cannot work, as there is no daily labor around the camps, and the aid has been stopped. She has to take care of her children and feed them and get them to school. She does not know how to do that now. She sighs when she admits: "I cannot feed my children well now." She also needs to feed her parents. This is impossible. She is trying to work on their farmland, which she and her family were forced to leave when they fled in 2011. The farm is almost four hours away from the camp, and going there requires paying for petrol and traveling through checkpoints. Therefore, her husband stays on the farm, and she commutes once per week between the farm and the camp, leaving her children to cook and care for themselves the days she is away. It is too expensive otherwise. She says: "My life has always been difficult." Nevertheless, she keeps on struggling for her children. "They are my hope," she says, showing a photo of a flower she explains signifies the beauty she wishes for their future (Hedström et al. 2023).

Hope and love for one's kin and the future materialize here as practice rather than as mere feelings or emotions. As bell hooks (2001, 13) puts it: "To think of love as an action, rather than a feeling" foregrounds the labor involved in sustaining hope and in making life worth living in the present. It is, to borrow from the climate scientist Lesley Head (2016, 11), "a gritty-keeping-on kind of hope." A mother of four explains: "After the coup, I feel like our lives have plunged into darkness." She pauses, then says: "I feel so depressed, but I can't be just sitting and doing nothing. I have to move on to carry out my family's responsibilities." Her friend, a mother of two, agrees with some defiance: "Yes, my life is more difficult now, but I have the courage to resist those challenges."

Imagining the intimate relations of everyday life as the locus of this hope allows us to see the political possibilities inherent in women's everyday labor. Militarized social reproduction is then more than physical labor, as the women in this book have taught us. (Re)produced from the household, women's emotional, symbolic, and material labor forges generational ties, linking past to present. This labor exists in relation both to the broader war effort and to the families and communities these women sustain, animating revolutionary life and hope for the future.

The Household, Gender Order(s), and War

By situating the household as an important, indeed key, aspect of warfare, this book has both built on and revised feminist research on militarization and political economy for conflict-affected contexts. Understanding the gendered household as a contributor to militarization demonstrates broader and deeper linkages between a gendered political-economic order—specifically a gendered division of labor (re)produced within the household—and the conduct of war. This enables a better understanding of the dynamics of gendered labor, the household, and war-making: how the gendered division of labor can both limit and potentially transform prevailing gender orders. Feminist political-economic research points to the importance of analyzing gendered structures in war-affected contexts (Cohn 2013; Kostovicova, Bojicic-Dzelilovic, and Henry 2020; Tanyag 2024; True and Tanyag 2017); this book adds an important dimension by highlighting the importance of social reproductive duties in making wars possible. Foregrounding militarized social reproduction alongside the household adds to existing contributions that underline the role of gender representations in conflict (Mookherjee 2015; D'Costa 2010). This emphasis also provides a novel way of understanding how political-economic relations of gender are implicated in the outbreak and continuation of conflict.

Feminist political-economic research on women and crisis demonstrates relationships between inequality and physical insecurity during and after crisis and armed conflict (Tanyag 2024; True 2012).This book builds on such research by proposing that insecurity in conflict must be understood in relationship to a gendered division of labor and the devaluation of women's reproductive and productive duties. As I have demonstrated here, gendered insecurity both results from militarization and serves to reinforce the centrality of the household in the conflict. Significantly, by introducing the concept of militarized social reproduction, this book inverts conflict analyses that render the household or women's labor solely domestic and, thus, irrelevant. Instead, it argues that the household is an inherently gendered, militarized, and political space that impacts, and is impacted by, the conflict contexts in which it exists.

In other words, Kachin women's experiences complicate simplistic portrayals of women as either victims or agents in war and help center the relationality of their labor, which both shapes and is shaped by the broader political economy of war. This is critical labor that helps maintain intimate bonds and relationships both outside and inside army life, sustaining struggle against as well as survival under the military junta today—but often at a high cost to the women themselves, as we saw in chapter 1.

Highlighting this relationship is critical for enabling more nuanced theorizations of the role gender plays in war. The question of why rebel wars break out and how they are fought occupies a lot of space in the study of civil wars, rebel governance, and military organization, not just in Myanmar studies but also more generally. The usual response to this question is to turn to military institutions or military leaders for answers, focusing on operational strength, strategies, tactics, and methods of fighting or the logistics of combat service support. Several studies emphasize the role ethnicity, religion, or ideology play in the outbreak of civil wars. I do not dispute that military strategies, logistics, or identity-based politics shape civil wars, but I also do not think such a focus can adequately explain how civil wars are fought and endured. Instead, I believe we need to capture the everyday lived experiences of war; by asking how wars are experienced, we might be able to better understand why they persist.

Examining the conflict from the experience of everyday women sheds new light on how the conflict is maintained and demonstrates how women have been, and continue to be, critical to the realization of military objectives. In Kachinland, the reliance of the armed apparatus on women's labor entrenches a gender order that sustains conflict while constraining women's material and emotional security, already precarious within the context of state oppression and attacks. Linking the household with gendered experiences of insecurity and war provides a useful framework for conceptualizing the impact of gender orders not just on women but also on the outbreak and conduct of conflict. In fact, the household, and, in particular, women's undervalued or unpaid militarized social reproductive duties, plays a key role in both legitimizing and sustaining conflict. Thus, trivializing women's extensive work undermines opportunities for alternative gender orders.

Arriving at this conclusion does not mean to assume that all women in Kachinland support military objectives, that the women who did support the KIO always did so intentionally, or that no women rejected their gendered roles and responsibilities. The household can be a space for both resistance and compliance, and the relationship between the household and war is neither deterministic nor unidirectional but dynamic and in process (see Chisholm 2022; Chisholm and Eichler 2018; Hyde 2024). However, within rebel groups that are engaged in long-term conflicts, like those in Myanmar, everyday life is experienced not only on the battlefield in direct conflict but also in the mundane rituals of household and community life (Arjona, Kasfir, and Mampilly 2015). This means that these everyday reproductive rituals form a critical dynamic of rebel conflict. While the specific circumstances of this labor may differ across temporal and geographical sites, a majority of this work is underpaid or unpaid, obscured from official accounts, and predominantly undertaken by women. In other words, one implication of these gendered norms, premised as they are on the notion that women are civilians and caretakers, is that they hide the extensive work women engage in. Centering militarized social reproduction in the analysis of rebel warfare therefore demonstrates how women's work sustains the military efforts of the rebel armed forces, and reveals how material, affective, and emotional ties to the nation are forged through women's labor, sacrifices, dedication, and, above all, their hopes for the future, even as jets attack their families.

In this book, I have attempted to recover the experiences of women mobilized for war across these different cycles by bringing to the forefront women's own recollections of living through war and centering their labor in an analysis of revolutionary politics and war-making. This has allowed me to show how women's labor and everyday experiences take shape in relation to both broader relations of state oppression and brutality and more local wartime gender orders. This focus has allowed me to move beyond the usual story of wars being fought between men on battlefields in order to highlight a story in which women are protagonists and actors and women's everyday labor is understood as a critical dynamic of military objectives and resistance efforts. This has helped me articulate a herstory of wartime labor and its significance to wartime orders.

This book is a feminist intervention that highlights the gendered dynamics of wartime economies and foregrounds the creativity, ambition, and strategies of the women involved in this work. While this book has focused on the specific experiences of Kachin women, its findings have implications for conflicts far beyond Myanmar. My research suggests that women's reproductive and productive work may also underpin conflict-affected communities and armed conflicts in other contexts.

As Cynthia Enloe (2017, 43) argues, war is never static. Neither is the gendered and militarized household. The experiences of the women examined in this book illustrate how gender relations of labor both impact and are impacted by protracted war. Scholarship or analysis that ignores this will produce incomplete findings. Taking seriously the gendered relations of power results in knowledge that recognizes and responds to the gendered structural inequalities shaping war. Analyzing the ways in which processes of militarization and war are imbricated in political-economic relations of gender is key to understanding how everyday labor informs the conduct of conflict. Interrogating the contradictions inherent in these gendered processes can help draw attention to possibilities for contestation, activism, and, ultimately, change. Thus, recognition of the household as a political and militarized space can enable a more nuanced analysis of how wars break out and endure as well as how they might end. Women's work, far from unimportant, carries with it the potential to both limit and transform prevailing gendered relations of power and, thus, war itself.

Notes

PREFACE

1. See, for example, Brenner 2019; Kiik 2016b; L Gum Ja Htung 2018; Lahtaw 2007; Lintner 1990; Oishi 2020; Williams 2017; Laoutides and Ware 2016.

2. For example, Findings from the First Round of the Myanmar Household Welfare Survey (2022) found that over 70 percent of the households in Kachin State reported no or reduced income as compared to the year before (IFPRI 2022).

INTRODUCTION

1. As detailed by a camp profile report undertaken on all IDP camps located in both Kachin and Northern Shan State, the majority (94 percent) of female camp residents were engaged in farming before displacement (CCCM Cluster and Joint IDP Profiling Service 2016).

2. Civil society and UN reports on displaced women and livelihood in Kachin State demonstrate similar findings. See, for example, Trocaire and Oxfam (2017) and UN Office for the Coordination of Humanitarian Affairs (2014). Moreover, as recent reports have noted, displacement means that access to land is restricted, increasing poverty and insecurity (Durable Peace Program Consortium 2018).

3. A report by Fortify Rights (2018), a human rights organization working in Southeast Asia, notes that after the return to war in 2011, the government of Myanmar "severely and systematically limited humanitarian access to displaced populations in Kachin State" by imposing unnecessarily onerous travel restrictions, making it all but impossible for some aid organizations to access displaced communities, and by directly threatening local health providers with prosecution if they continued to deliver aid to areas under the control of the KIO/KIA. After the coup in 2021, the possibility for aid delivery has narrowed even further, with some local aid providers hiding their supplies and others opting to not deliver aid to KIO/KIA-controlled areas due to fear of repercussion by the military regime, including killings and arrests of local staff (Fishbein and Lusan 2021).

4. Similar to Wungpawng, Shanland and Kawthoolei are used by Shan and Karen nationalists and political movements to represent their historical homelands, signifying their aspiration for self-determination.

5. The so-called spirit of the Panglong Agreement is an issue of interpretation that has been used by different political groups across the years, most recently at the Twenty-First Century Panglong Conference, which kick-started the (much-critiqued) peace process in 2016. For more information about the Panglong Agreement, the notion of the "spirit," and the ways in which spirit has been deployed by politicians across the years, see Sadan (2013, 273).

6. Major N'Chyaw Tang (n.d., 37) recalls Colonel Zau Seng's speech at the first raising of the flag, on December 24, 1962: "The red colour is symbolising the bravery and audacious fighting spirit of the Kachin, the green colour representing the jade and gold resourceful and peaceful nature of Kachinland. The sword cross is illustrating of the Kachin using of the swords and spears as their staple weaponries from generation to generation and its white colour representing the honesty, loyal and humbly mind of the Kachins."

7. This has been widely commented upon, and I am here learning from studies and research published by, among others: Jones (2016); Kachin Development Networking Group (2012); Kiik (2016a); L Gum Ja Htung (2018); and Woods (2011).

8. According to the 2017 Humanitarian Response Plan, 77 percent of displaced people in Kachin State are women and their dependents (UN Office for the Coordination of Humanitarian Affairs 2017). The 2018 Interim Humanitarian Response Plan puts this figure at 76 percent; in Northern Shan at 78 percent (Linn 2016; Martow 2015; UN Office for the Coordination of Humanitarian Affairs 2016). In 2020, these numbers had risen to 82 percent (UN Women 2021). These figures do not take into account the most recent displacements, after the coup in early 2021.

9. Aid has been blocked primarily from reaching camps in KIO-controlled areas where around half of displaced people reside (United Nations Development Programme 2015). A recent report released by the United Nations Development Programme notes that poverty, already dire, is increasing in Kachin State, including in areas not affected by the fighting: the IHLCA estimates that about 29 percent of the population in Kachin State are living below the poverty line (UN Office for the Coordination of Humanitarian Affairs 2017).

10. I am grateful to Dominique Dillabough-Lefebvre for sharing his work on insurgent kinship among the Karen in Brigade 5.

1. CARE, LOVE, AND DEPLETION IN DISPLACEMENT

1. See also Project Maje's (1995) report on women in the KIA, in which all women interviewed, whether active soldiers or not, were engaged in unpaid or underpaid subsistence and reproductive work duties. Similarly, a 2017 report on women in displacement camps found that among the 107 women interviewed, nearly all were listed as "dependents" on their family registration card, suggesting that household work is not counted as formal work (Trocaire and Oxfam 2017). The research undertaken for this study echoes these findings for liberated areas.

2. Another complicating factor is that, according to my research interlocutors, when schools closed down across Myanmar due to COVID-19, many students came to schools in KIO-controlled areas, where the number of students soon superseded the classrooms and dormitories available. This also contributed to a COVID-19 outbreak in these areas and increased security by KIO officials who tried to contain the outbreak. See also *Kachin News Group* 2020.

3. See Durable Peace Program Consortium 2018; Durable Peace Programme Consortium 2020; Maung 2019; Sarma, Rippa, and Dean 2023; UNCHR and UNDP 2018.

4. Displaced women report having only enough savings to last their families for just under a week. Worryingly, this number of days is half the number reported by women who were asked the same questions in 2015, suggesting that economic insecurity in displacement camps has increased over time (Durable Peace Programme Consortium 2020).

5. See Refugees International 2017; UN Women 2021.

2. THE POLITICAL ECONOMY OF THE REVOLUTIONARY HOUSEHOLD

1. See Jocelyn Viterna (2013) for a similar discussion about women mobilized for war in El Salvador.

2. As noted with other revolutionary movements, when femininity is mobilized to render military movements legitimate, it provides little or no real room for change: women enter public spaces in roles reinforcing the gender order, for example as dutiful daughters or as romanticized victims. See, for example, Swati Parashar's (2014) work on

women active in the Kashmir conflict and Srila Roy's (2012) excellent study on the Maoist armed movement in India.

3. Officially known as the War Fund, it was often simply translated as "food costs," or *lu sha jahpu*.

4. As estimated by the 1973 Census (Maung 1986). See also Asia Justice and Rights 2015.

5. In the 1973 Census (Maung 1986), more than twice as many women as men were divorced or widowed. This number increased to three times as many once women reached the age of sixty (14). The vulnerability this generates for women is still an issue today. The KWAT also notes that the fact that women cannot traditionally inherit puts vulnerable women (widows or wives of abusive husbands) in precarious situations (Kachin Women's Association Thailand 2014).

6. The historian Mandy Sadan (2014) has recorded an oral history of her mother-in-law engaging in trading among China, Myitkyina, and Hpakant. Her gendered responsibilities were extensive. Sadan writes that her mother-in-law "had to find ways of providing for everybody—her own children and the many others she looked after, including the score of associated relatives who bedded down in the house for months at a time" (44).

7. See also Nhkum Bu Lu's (2016) rich oral history, which recounts her experience of engaging in trade during the conflict years.

8. As the KWA formally comes under the KIO's CC, the CC must approve its activities. The CC can also make decisions about the strategic direction of the organization.

9. In these areas, the KIO offers school education that is aligned with the Burmese educational system so as to ensure opportunities for Kachin students to study at universities across Myanmar. After the war began, this changed, as matriculation exams at schools run by the KIO are no longer recognized by the Burmese government (Htet Khaung Linn 2016; Jolliffe 2014).

10. It is difficult to collect precise data on when exactly military initiatives begin or end, as this exchange with a military leader responsible for military recruitments explains: "I don't quite remember the year, but I believe it was around 2009 / 2010 when we started accepting female officers, but I don't remember the exact year. But it was definitely before the war resumed in 2011, because when the war broke out, the male students mid-training went to the front line, and the females stayed behind to provide support."

11. For more background information on the KIA's military training programs, see the report by Child Soldiers International (2015) detailing child recruitment practices. This report highlights military-funded education, "corrective" recruitment for drug addicts and household quotas.

12. See Fieseler, Hampf, and Schwarzkopf (2014) for a discussion on how changes in wartime gender orders in the UK, the US, and the Soviet Union shaped women's involvment in the military and their access (or lack of) to combat positions.

3. WOMEN'S MILITARY CONSCRIPTION IN KACHINLAND

1. As Maria Stern and Sanna Strand (2021, 9) put it: "The seemingly disproportionate amount of scholarly (often medical) research and government regulations that focus on the management of women's bodies and fluids in military contexts, compared to non-female-specific bodily fluids such as sweat and diarrhea, and the blood that seeps or gushes from bodily wounds inflicted in battle, is noteworthy in this regard."

2. The code of conduct also regulates rape. As gleaned from the interview data, this seems to be the only form of gender-based violence recognized by the army. Perpetrators of rape are demoted and sentenced to a maximum of 120 days of hard labor.

3. In Burmese, မယားငယ် or အပျိုတော်မယ် translates to "small wives/girls."

4. AS TOUGH AS MEN

1. There is scant literature available (in English) detailing the activities and particularities of the EEDY. Ashley South (2008) states that the training began in 2002 and that between 2002 and 2007, more than four thousand students graduated from the program; a report by Child Soldiers International (2015) notes that the program began in 2003; and an article published by the Kachin New Group mentions 2004 as the commencement of the program (Lahpai 2010). My information, that the EEDY program began in 2003 and has had a total of 3,780 graduates, is based on field research and interviews with participants in the program as well as written communication with an adviser to the KIO's CC who shared the total breakdown of student numbers with me. As this came from the organizers of the program, I am using these numbers.

2. I am here of course drawing on Bina Agarwal's (1997) work on intrahousehold bargaining but am extending it to households in war.

3. This finding echoes Leena Vastapuu's (2018) research on girl soldiers in the Liberian Civil War, suggesting that rank in some cases trumps gender.

5. WEDDINGS AMID WAR

Thank you to Bart Klem for suggesting the title of this chapter, and to Marika Sosnowski for your careful feedback on the legal identity aspects of this chapter. I am also grateful to Laur Kiik for his insights regarding Kachin identity politics and practice.

1. As Major N'Chyaw Tang (n.d., 58) noted in his unpublished memoir: "The modification of the polity, the Title of the Jinghpaw have been a changed into the new one (Wunpawng) ethnic composition, Jinghpaw, Maru, La Shi, Azi, Lisu and Ravang, the ruling system by the chiefs and the Dowries paying and demands in this marriage system has been abolished off."

2. Weddings are also held in the brigades, but I have not obtained the numbers for these.

CONCLUSION

1. In 2011, the government was spending a mere 1.8 percent.

2. SIPRI 2023.

3. Defense spending increased from 10 to 12 percent. Education decreased from 8.4 to 7 percent; health 4.2 to 2.8 percent; and welfare was 0.5 to 0.3 percent. See UNOCHA 2022.

References

Abu-Lughod, Lila. 1993. *Writing Women's Worlds: Bedouin Stories*. 2008 ed. Berkeley: University of California Press.

Agarwal, Bina. 1997. "'Bargaining' and Gender Relations: Within and Beyond the Household." *Feminist Economics* 3 (1): 1–51. https://doi.org/10.1080/135457097338799.

Åhäll, Linda. 2012. "Motherhood, Myth and Gendered Agency." *International Feminist Journal of Politics* 14 (1): 37–41. https://doi.org/10.1080/14616742.2011.619781.

Ahmed, Sara. 2017. *Living a Feminist Life*. Durham, NC: Duke University Press.

Akawa, Martha, and Bience Gawanas. 2014. *The Gender Politics of the Namibian Liberation Struggle*. Basel, Switzerland: Basler Afrika Bibliographien.

Alison, Miranda. 2009. *Women and Political Violence: Female Combatants in Ethno-National Conflict*. London: Routledge.

Al-Khalili, Charlotte. 2023. *Waiting for the Revolution to End Syrian Displacement, Time and Subjectivity*. London: University College London Press.

Andaya, Barbara Watson. 2020. "Rethinking the Historical Place of 'Warrior Women' in Southeast Asia." In *Women Warriors in Southeast Asia*. Abingdon, UK: Routledge.

Arjona, Ana, Nelson Kasfir, and Zachariah Mampilly, eds. 2015. *Rebel Governance in Civil War*. New York: Cambridge University Press.

Asal, Victor, and Amira Jadoon. 2020. "When Women Fight: Unemployment, Territorial Control and the Prevalence of Female Combatants in Insurgent Organizations." *Dynamics of Asymmetric Conflict* 13 (3): 258–81. https://doi.org/10.1080/17467586.2019.1700542.

Asia Justice and Rights. 2015. "Open the Box: Women's Experiences of War, Peace and Impunity in Myanmar." Jakarta: AJAR.

Baines, Erin. 2014. "Forced Marriage as a Political Project: Sexual Rules and Relations in the Lord's Resistance Army." *Journal of Peace Research* 51 (3): 405–17. https://doi.org/10.1177/0022343313519666.

Baines, Erin. 2016. *Buried in the Heart: Women, Complex Victimhood and the War in Northern Uganda*. Cambridge, UK: Cambdrige University Press.

Bedford, Kate, and Shirin M. Rai. 2010. "Feminists Theorize International Political Economy." *Signs* 36 (1): 1–18. https://doi.org/10.1086/652910.

Belak, Brenda. 2002. *Gathering Strength: Women from Burma on Their Rights*. Chiang Mai, Thailand: Images Asia.

Berry, Marie E., and Milli Lake. 2021. "Women's Rights after War: On Gender Interventions and Enduring Hierarchies." *Annual Review of Law and Social Sciences* 17 (1): 459–81.

Bhattacharya, Tithi, ed. 2017. *Social Reproduction Theory: Remapping Class, Recentering Oppression*. London: Pluto.

Blackburn, Susan, and Helen Ting, eds. 2013. *Women in Southeast Asian Nationalist Movements: A Biograhical Approach*. Singapore: National University of Singapore Press.

Brenner, David. 2019. *Rebel Politics: A Political Sociology of Armed Struggle in Myanmar's Borderlands*. Ithaca, NY: Cornell University Press.

Buchanan, John. 2019. "Security Integration Efforts in Myanmar (1945–2010): A Historical Overview." Institute for Strategy and Policy—Myanmar.

Carreiras, Helena. 2006. *Gender and the Military: Women in the Armed Forces of Western Democracies*. Cass Military Studies. London: Routledge.

CCCM Cluster and Joint IDP Profiling Service. 2016. "Myanmar Kachin and Northern Shan States Camp Profiling Rounds 1–3: Cross-Camp and Trend Analysis Report 2013–2016." Yangon.

Central Statistical Organization (CSO) UNDP and World Bank. 2020. "Myanmar Living Conditions Survey 2017: Socio-Economic Report." Nay Pyi Taw: Ministry of Planning, Finance and Industry, UNDP and WB.

Child Soldiers International. 2015. "A Dangerous Refuge: Ongoing Child Recruitment by the Kachin Independence Army." *A Dangerous Refuge: Ongoing Child Recruitment by the Kachin Independence Army*. London. https://doi.org/10.1007/s13398-014-0173-7.2.

Chisholm, Amanda. 2022. *The Gendered and Colonial Lives of Gurkhas in Private Security from Military to Market*. Edinburgh, Scotland: Edinburgh University Press.

Chisholm, Amanda, and Maya Eichler. 2018. "Reproductions of Global Security: Accounting for the Private Security Household." *International Feminist Journal of Politics* 4 (20): 563–82.

Chua, Lynette J. 2019. *The Politics of Love in Myanmar LGBT Mobilization and Human Rights as a Way of Life*. Palo Alto, CA: Stanford University Press.

Cockburn, Cynthia. 2010. "Gender Relations as Causal in Militarization and War," *International Feminist Journal of Politics* 12 (2): 37–41. https://doi.org/10.1080/14616741003665169.

Cohn, Carol, ed. 2013. *Women and Wars: Contested Histories, Uncertain Futures*. Malden, MA: Polity.

Collier, Paul, and Anke Hoeffler. 2002. "On the Incidence of Civil War in Africa." *Journal of Conflict Resolution* 46 (1): 13–28. https://doi.org/10.1177/0022002702046001002.

Collier, Paul, and Nicholas Sambanis, eds. 2005. *Understanding Civil War*. Vol. 1. Washington, DC: World Bank Group.

Dagens Nyheter. 2017. "1.768 kvinnor i försvaret: 'Alla anmälningar om övergrepp och kränkningar måste tas på allvar.'" *Dagens Nyheter*, sec. DN Debatt. https://www.dn.se/debatt/1768-kvinnor-i-forsvaret-alla-anmalningar-maste-tas-pa-allvar/.

Dean, Karin. 2005. "Spaces and Territorialities on the Sino-Burmese Boundary: China, Burma and the Kachin." *Political Geography* 24 (7): 808–30.

D'Costa, Bina. 2010. *Nationbuilding, Gender and War Crimes in South Asia*. London: Routledge.

Department of Defense. 2023. "Annual Report on Sexual Harassment and Violence at the Military Service Academies: Academic Program Year 2021–2022." US Department of Defense. https://www.sapr.mil/sites/default/files/public/docs/reports/MSA/DOD_Annual_Report_on_Sexual_Harassment_and_Violence_at_MSAs_APY21-22.pdf.

DeVault, Marjorie, and Glenda Gross. 2012. "Feminist Qualitative Interviewing: Experience, Talk, and Knowledge." In *Handbook of Feminist Research: Theory and Praxis*, edited by Sharlene Nagy Hesse-biber, 206–36. Los Angeles: Sage. https://doi.org/10.1111/j.1469-0691.2011.03558.x/pdf.

De Volo, Lorraine Bayard. 2018. *Women and the Cuban Insurrection: How Gender Shaped Castro's Victory*. Cambridge, UK: Cambridge University Press.

Diao, Ying. 2021. "Traditional Culture as a Vehicle for Christian Future-Making Ethnic Minority Elites Pioneering Representation in Northern Myanmar." *Social Anthropology* 29: 669–85.

Dillabough-Lefebvre, Dominique. 2025. "Insurgent Kinship: The Paradoxes of Autonomy and Dependence in the Karen Highlands of Southeastern Myanmar." PhD thesis, London School of Economics and Political Science.

Douglass, Mike. 2012. "Global Householding and Social Reproduction: Migration Research, Dynamics and Public Policy in East and Southeast Asia." ARI Working Paper Series. Singapore: National University of Singapore.

Dowling, Emma. 2016. "Blog Love's Labour's Cost: The Political Economy of Intimacy." London: Verso. http://www.versobooks.com/blogs/2499-love-s-labour-s-cost-the-political-economy-of-intimacy.

Duncanson, Claire, and Rachel Woodward. 2015. "Regendering the Military: Theorizing Women's Military Participation." *Security Dialogue* 47 (1). https://doi.org/10.1177/0967010615614137.

Durable Peace Programme Consortium. 2018. "Displaced and Dispossessed: Conflict-Affected Communities and Their Land of Origin in Kachin State, Myanmar." https://www.oxfam.org/en/research/displaced-and-dispossessed-conflict-affected-communities-and-their-land-origin-kachin.

Durable Peace Programme Consortium. 2020. "Displaced Women's Experiences, Opportunities and Priorities in Kachin State."

Elfenbein, Rachel. 2019. *Engendering Revolution: Women, Unpaid Labour, and Maternalism in Bolivarian Venezuela*. Austin: University of Texas Press.

Elias, Juanita, and Samanthi J. Gunawardana. 2013. *The Global Political Economy of the Household in Asia*. Basingstoke, UK: Palgrave Macmillan. https://doi.org/10.1057/9781137338907.

Elias, Juanita, and Shirin Rai. 2015. "The Everyday Gendered Political Economy of Violence." *Politics & Gender* 11 (2): 424–29. https://doi.org/10.1017/S1743923X15000148.

Elliot, Patricia. 1999. *The White Umbrella: A Woman's Struggle for Freedom in Burma*. Bangkok, Thailand: Friends Books.

Elshtain, Jean Bethke. 1987. *Women and War*. New York: Basic Books.

Enloe, Cynthia. 2000. *Maneuvers: The International Politics of Militarizing Women's Lives*. Berkeley: University of California Press.

Enloe, Cynthia. 2010. *Nimo's War, Emma's War: Making Feminist Sense of the Iraq War*. Berkeley: University of California Press.

Enloe, Cynthia. 2017. *The Big Push: Exposing and Challenging the Persistence of Patriarchy*. Oakland: University of California Press.

Eriksson-Baaz, Maria, and Maria Stern. 2013. *Sexual Violence as a Weapon of War? Perceptions, Prescriptions, Problems in the Congo and Beyond*. London: Zed Books.

Euro Burma Office (EBO). 2010. The Kachins' Dilemma—Become a Border Guard Force or Return to Warfare. EBO Analysis Paper No. 2. Brussels: EBO.

Evans, Brad, and Gayatri Chakravorty Spivak. 2016. "When Law Is Not Justice." *New York Times*, July 13. https://www.nytimes.com/2016/07/13/opinion/when-law-is-not-justice.html.

Faxon, Hilary Oliva. 2020. "Securing Meaningful Life: Women's Work and Land Rights in Rural Myanmar." *Journal of Rural Studies* 76, 76–84. https://doi.org/10.1016/j.jrurstud.2020.03.011.

Federici, Silvia. 2004. *Caliban and the Witch*. 2014 ed. New York: Autonmedia.

Federici, Silvia. 2012. *Revolution at Point Zero: Housework, Reproduction, and Feminist Struggle*. Oakland, CA: PM.

Federici, Silvia. 2019. "Social Reproduction Theory: History, Issues and Present Challenges." *Radical Philosophy* 2 (4): 55–58.

Ferguson, Jane. 2013. "Is the Pen Mightier than the AK-47? Tracking Shan Women's Militancy Within and Beyond." *Intersections: Gender and Sexuality in Asia and the Pacific*, no. 33, 1–12.

Ferguson, Jane. 2021. *Repossessing Shanland Myanmar, Thailand, and a Nation-State Deferred*. Madison: University of Wisconsin Press.

Fieseler, Beate, M. Michaela Hampf, and Jutta Schwarzkopf. 2014. "Gendering Combat: Military Women's Status in Britain, the United States, and the Soviet Union during the Second World War." *Women's Studies International Forum* 47, 115–26. https://doi.org/10.1016/j.wsif.2014.06.011.

Fink, Christina. 2001. *Living Silence in Burma: Surviving under Military Rule*. London: Zed Books.

Fishbein, Emily, and Nu Nu Lusan. 2021. "'From Complex to Chaotic': Myanmar Coup Shrinks Frontline Aid." *New Humanitarian*, May 3. Accessed September 23, 2024. https://www.thenewhumanitarian.org/fr/node/262002.

Fortify Rights. 2018. "'They Block Everything': Avoidable Deprivations in Humanitarian Aid to Ethnic Civilians Displaced by War in Kachin State, Myanmar." Bangkok. Accessed September 23, 2024. https://www.fortifyrights.org/downloads/They_Block_Everything_EN_Fortify_Rights_August_2018.pdf.

Fortin, Katharine, Bart Klem, and Marika Sosnowski. 2021. "Legal Identity and Rebel Governance: A Comparative Perspective on Lived Consequence of Contested Sovereignty." In *Statelessness, Governance, and the Problem of Citizenship*. Manchester, UK: Manchester University Press.

Fraser, Nancy. 2017. "Crisis of Care? On the Social-Reproductive Contradictions of Contemporary Capitalism." In *Social Reproduction Theory: Remapping Class, Recentering Oppression*, edited by Tithi Bhattacharya. London: Pluto.

Fujii, Lee Ann. 2009. *Killing Neighbors: Webs of Violence in Rwanda*. Ithaca, NY: Cornell University Press.

Fujii, Lee Ann. 2010. "Shades of Truth and Lies: Interpreting Testimonies of War and Violence." *Journal of Peace Research* 47 (2): 231–41. https://doi.org/10.1177/0022343309353097.

Fujii, Lee Ann. 2012. "Research Ethics 101: Dilemmas and Responsibilities." *PS—Political Science and Politics* 45 (4): 717–23. https://doi.org/10.1017/S1049096512000819.

Garbagni, Giulia, and Matthew J. Walton. 2020. "Imagining Kawthoolei: Strategies of Petitioning for Karen Statehood in Burma in the First Half of the 20th Century." *Nations and Nationalism* 26 (3): 759–74. https://doi.org/10.1111/nana.12613.

Gender Equality Network. 2013. "Women's Needs Assessment in IDP Camps, Kachin State." Yangon: Gender Equality Network.

Global Witness. 2015. "Jade: Myanmar's 'Big State Secret.'" October 23. London. https://www.globalwitness.org/en/campaigns/oil-gas-and-mining/myanmarjade/.

Guillemin, Marilys, and Lynn Gillam. 2004. "Ethics, Reflexivity, and 'Ethically Important Moments' in Research." *Qualitative Inquiry* 10 (2): 261–80. https://doi.org/10.1177/1077800403262360.

Gunawardana, Samanthi. 2016. "'To Finish, We Must Finish': Everyday Practices of Depletion in Sri Lankan Export-Processing Zones." *Globalizations* 13 (6): 861–75. https://doi.org/10.1080/14747731.2016.1155341.

Haokip, Seilienmang. 2023. "Memory and Kinship across the Indo–Myanmar Border: A Study of the Lived Experiences of Displaced Kuki Families." *Memory Studies*. https://doi.org/10.1177/17506980231188484.

Harding, Sandra. 1992. "After the Neutrality Ideal: Science, Politics, and 'Strong Objectivity.'" *Social Research* 59 (3): 567–87.

Harriden, Jessica. 2012. *The Authority of Influence: Women and Power in Burmese History*. Copenhagen, Denmark: NIAS.

Head, Lesley. 2016. *Hope and Grief in the Anthropocene: Re-Conceptualising Human–Nature Relations*. Abingdon, UK: Routledge.

Hedström, Jenny. 2016. "'Before I Joined the Army, I Was Like a Child' Militarism and Women's Rights in Kachinland." In *War and Peace in the Borderlands of Myanmar:*

The Kachin Ceasefire, 1994–2011, edited by Mandy Sadan, 236–56. Copenhagen, Denmark: NIAS.

Hedström, Jenny. 2018. "Confusion, Seduction, Failure: Emotions as Reflexive Knowledge in Conflict Settings." *International Studies Review* 21 (4): 1–16. https://doi .org/10.1093/isr/viy063.

Hedström, Jenny, Hilary Oliva Faxon, Zin Mar Phyo, Htoi Pan, Moe Kha Yae, Ka Yay, and Mi Mi. 2023. "Forced Fallow Fields: Making Meaningful Life in the Myanmar Spring Revolution." *Civil Wars*. https://doi.org/10.1080/13698249.2023.2240620.

Herbert, Melissa S. 1998. *Camouflage Isn't Only for Combat: Gender, Sexuality and Women in the Military*. New York: New York University Press.

Hewamanne, Sandya. 2016. *Sri Lanka's Global Factory Workers (Un) Disciplined Desires and Sexual Struggles in a Post-Colonial Society*. London: Routledge.

Hnin Wai. 2024. "Struggles of a Woman Armed Revolutionary." *Independent Journal of Burmese Scholarship*, Special Issue on Feminism, 4 (5): 172–79.

Hoang, Kimberly Kay. 2015. *Dealing in Desire: Asian Ascendancy, Western Decline, and the Hidden Currencies of Global Sex Work*. Oakland: University of California Press.

hooks, bell. 2001. *All about Love: New Visions*. New York: William Morrow.

Howell, Alison. 2015. "Making War Work: Resilience, Emotional Fitness, and Affective Economies in Western Militaries." In *Emotions, Politics and War*, edited by Linda Åhäll and Thomas Gregory, 141–54. London: Routledge.

Htet Khaung Linn. 2016. "Amid War, Kachin Rebels Expand Education System for IDPs." *Mizzima News*, July 30. https://www.mizzima.com/news-features/amid-war -kachin-rebels-expand-education-system-idps.

Htet Khaung Linn. 2016. "Exhausted by War, Kachin IDPs in Rebel Areas See Aid Dwindle." *Myanmar Now*, July 8. https://www.frontiermyanmar.net/en/exhausted-by -war-kachin-idps-in-rebel-areas-see-aid-dwindle/.

Human Rights Watch. 1992. "Burma." In *World Report 1992*, 347–48. New York: Human Rights Watch.

Hyde, Alexandra. 2024. *Regimented Life: An Ethnography of Army Wives*. Edinburgh, Scotland: Edinburgh University Press.

IFPRI. 2022. "Welfare and Vulnerability: Findings from the First Round of the Myanmar Household Welfare Survey." HOUSEHOLD- AND COMMUNITY-LEVEL SURVEYS. 0 ed. Washington, DC: International Food Policy Research Institute. https://doi.org/10.2499/p15738coll2.135931.

Ikeya, Chie. 2011. *Refiguring Women, Colonialism, and Modernity in Burma*. Honolulu: University of Hawai'i Press.

Integrated Household Living Conditions Survey in Myanmar (IHLCA). 2011. Poverty Profile: Kachin State. United Nations Development Programme (UNDP) and Myanmar Ministry of National Planning and Economic Development. https:// www.mm.undp.org.

International Crisis Group. 2013. "A Tentative Peace in Myanmar's Kachin Conflict." Yangon: International Crisis Group. http://www.crisisgroup.org/~/media/Files/asia /south-east-asia/burma-myanmar/b140-a-tentative-peace-in-myanmars-kachin -conflict.

Ismael Khin Maung. 1986. "The Population of Burma: An Analysis of the 1973 Census." *Papers—East-West Population Institute*. Vol. 97. Hamilton Library, University of Hawai'i at Manoa.

Johns Hopkins Bloomberg School of Public Health and Kachin Women's Association Thailand. 2018. "Estimating Trafficking of Myanmar Women for Forced Marriage and Childbearing in China." Baltimore. Accessed September 23, 2024.

https://reliefweb.int/report/china/estimating-trafficking-myanmar-women -forced-marriage-and-childbearing-china.

Johnston, Melissa, and Jayanthi Lingham. 2020. "Inclusive Economies, Enduring Peace in Myanmar and Sri Lanka: Field Report." Melbourne, Australia: Monash University.

Jolliffe, Kim. 2014. *Ethnic Conflict and Social Services in Myanmar's Contested Regions.* Yankin, Myanmar: Asia Foundation (Burma).

Jones, Lee. 2016. "Understanding Myanmar's Ceasefires: Geopolitics, Political Economy and State-Building." In *War and Peace in the Borderlands of Myanmar: The Kachin Ceasefire, 1994–2011*, edited by Mandy Sadan, 95–113. Copenhagen, Denmark: NIAS.

Kachin Development Networking Group. 2012. "Lessons from the Kachin 'Development' Experience." KNDG. https://kdng.org/wp-content/uploads/2012/05/Lessonsfrom Kachindevelopmentexperience-92012-English.pdf

Kachin News Group. 2020. "Burma Army Destroys KIO COVID-19 Screening Point." June 24. https://kachinnews.com/2020/06/24/burma-army-destroys-kio-covid -19-screening-point/.

Kachin Women's Association Thailand. 2014. "Silent Offensive: How Burma Army Strategies Are Fuelling the Kachin Drug Crisis." Chiang Mai: KWAT.

Karen Women's Organisation. 2010. "Walking amongst Sharp Knives. The Unsung Courage of Karen Women Village Chiefs in Conflict Areas of Eastern Burma." Mae Sariang: KWO.

Khin Su Kyi. 2019. "Saw Mra Razar Lin, a Political Traveler in the Midst of Challenges" [in Burmese: ပူလဆောင်မှတွေကြေကြ နိုင်ငံရေးခရီးသည် စတေမြှရာဇာလင်း]." *Honest Information.* https://hiburma.net/2019/12/ပူလဆောင်မှတွေကြေကြ-နှိc/.

Kiik, Laur. 2016a. "Conspiracy, God's Plan, and National Emergency: Kachin Popular Analyses of the Ceasefire Era and Its Resource Grabs." In *War and Peace in the Borderlands of Myanmar: The Kachin Ceasefire, 1994–2011*, edited by Mandy Sadan, 205–35. Copenhagen, Denmark: NIAS.

Kiik, Laur. 2016b. "Nationalism and Anti-Ethno-Politics: Why 'Chinese Development' Failed at Myanmar's Myitsone Dam." *Eurasian Geography and Economics* 57 (3): 374–402. https://doi.org/10.1080/15387216.2016.1198265.

Kirby, Paul. 2020. "The Body Weaponized: War, Sexual Violence and the Uncanny." *Security Dialogue* 51 (2–3): 211–30. https://doi.org/10.1177/0967010619895663.

Kostovicova, Denisa, Vesna Bojicic-Dzelilovic, and Marsha Henry. 2020. "Drawing on the Continuum: A War and Post-War Political Economy of Gender-Based Violence in Bosnia and Herzegovina." *International Feminist Journal of Politics* 22 (2): 250–72. https://doi.org/10.1080/14616742.2019.1692686.

Lahpai, Naw Din. 2010. "KIO Declares War against Drugs before Burma Elections." *Kachin News Group.* October 12. https://www.bnionline.net/en/kachin-news -group/item/9522-kio-declares-war-against-drugs-before-burma-elections -html.

Lahtaw, Ja Nan. 2007. "Peace Initiatives among Ethnic Nationalities: The Kachin Case." In *State, Society and Ethnicity*, edited by N. Ganesan and Kyaw Yin Hlaing, 236–55. Singapore: ISEAS. https://doi.org/10.1355/9789812307224-012.

Lanau, Roi Aung. 2009. "Kachin Borderlanders: A Case Study of Laiza Town along the Yunnan-Myanmar Frontier Area." Master's thesis, Chiang Mai University.

Lal, Jayati. 1999. "Situating Locations: The Politics of Self, Identity and 'Other' in Living and Writing the Text." In *Feminist Approaches to Theory and Methodology*, edited by Sharlene Hesse-Biber, Christina Gilmartin, and Robin Lydenberg, 100–37. New York: Oxford University Press.

Lanzona, Vina, and Frederik Rettig, eds. 2020. *Women Warriors in Southeast Asia*. Abingdon, UK: Routledge.

Laoutides, Costas, and Anthony Ware. 2016. "Reexamining the Centrality of Ethnic Identity to the Kachin Conflict." In *Conflict in Myanmar: War, Politics, Religion*, edited by Nick Cheesman and Nicholas Farrelly, 47–66. Lectures, Workshops, and Proceedings of International Conferences. ISEAS–Yusof Ishak Institute. https://www.cambridge.org/core/product/73E9223A8FF9D6B801728E20F118D58C.

Lebra, Joyce Chapman. 2008. *Women against the Raj: The Rhani of Jhansi Regiment*. Singapore: ISEAS.

L Gum Ja Htung. 2018. *Land Grabbing as a Process of State-Building in Kachin Areas, North Shan State, Myanmar*. Chiang Mai, Thailand: Chiang Mai University Press.

Li, Quan, and Ming Wen. 2005. "The Immediate and Lingering Effects of Armed Conflict on Adult Mortality: A Time-Series Cross-National Analysis." *Journal of Peace Research* 42 (4): 471–92. https://doi.org/10.1177/0022343305054092.

Lintner, Bertil. 1990. *Land of Jade: A Journey through Insurgent Burma*. Bangkok, Thailand: Orchid.

Lintner, Bertil. 2000. "The Golden Triangle Opium Trade: An Overview." Chiang Mai, Thailand: Asia Pacific Media Services.

Lomsky-Feder, Edna, and Orna Sasson-Levy. 2015. "Serving the Army as Secretaries: Intersectionality, Multi-Level Contract and Subjective Experience of Citizenship: Serving the Army as Secretaries." *British Journal of Sociology* 66 (1): 173–92. https://doi.org/10.1111/1468-4446.12102.

MacKenzie, Megan, Eda Gunaydin, and Umeya Chaudhuri. 2020. "Illicit Military Behavior as Exceptional and Inevitable: Media Coverage of Military Sexual Violence and the 'Bad Apples' Paradox." *International Studies Quarterly* 64 (1): 45–56. https://doi.org/10.1093/isq/sqz093.

MacKenzie, Megan H. 2015. *Beyond the Band of Brothers: The US Military and the Myth That Women Can't Fight*. Cambridge, UK: Cambridge University Press.

Mahmood, Saba. 2001. "Feminist Theory, Embodiment, and the Docile Agent: Some Reflections on the Egyptian Islamic Revival." *Cultural Anthropology* 16 (2): 202–36. https://doi.org/10.1525/can.2001.16.2.202.

Mahmood, Saba. 2005. *Politics of Piety: The Islamic Revivial and the Feminist Subject*. Princeton, NJ: Princeton University Press.

Mama, Amina, and Margo Okazawa-Rey. 2012. "Militarism, Conflict and Women's Activism in the Global Era: Challenges and Prospects for Women in Three West African Contexts." *Feminist Review* 101 (1): 97–123. https://doi.org/10.1057/fr.2011.57.

Manny Maung. 2019. "Internally Displaced Kachin Battle to Return Home." *Bangkok Post*, October 12. https://www.hrw.org/news/2019/10/12/internally-displaced-kachin-battle-return-home.

Maran La Raw. 2007. "On the Continuing Relevance of E. R. Leach's Political Systems of Highland Burma to Kachin Studies." In *Social Dynamics in the Highlands of Southeast Asia: Reconsidering Political Systems of Highland Burma*, edited by François Robinne and Mandy Sadan, 31–66. Leiden, The Netherlands: Brill.

Martow, Seamus. 2015. "Army Restrictions Leave Kachin Refugees without Aid." *The Irrawaddy*. August 21. https://www.irrawaddy.com/news/burma/army-restrictions-leave-kachin-refugees-without-aid.html.

Matfess, Hilary. 2024. *In Love and at War: Marriage in Non-State Armed Group*. Cambridge, UK: Cambridge University Press.

Mies, Maria. 2014. *Patriarchy and Accumulation on a World Scale: Women in the International Division of Labour*. London: Zed Books.

Mookherjee, Nayanika. 2015. *The Spectral Wound: Sexual Violence, Public Memories, and the Bangladesh War of 1971*. Durham, NC: Duke University Press.

Myanmar Department of Population. 2015a. "The 2014 Myanmar Population and Housing Census: Highlights of the Main Results." Ministry of Immigration and Population. Vol. 2-A. Nay Pyi Taw, Republic of the Union of Myanmar.

Myanmar Department of Population. 2015b. "The 2014 Myanmar Population and Housing Census: The Union Report." Vol. 2. Nay Pyi Taw, Republic of the Union of Myanmar.

Myanmar Department of Population. 2016. "The 2014 Myanmar Population and Housing Census. The Union Report: Occupation and Industry." Vol. 2-B. Nay Pyi Taw, Republic of the Union of Myanmar. https://data.unhcr.org/thailand/download .php?id=421.

N'Chyaw Tang. n.d. "Hidden Genocide Practice of Burman and Diary of Major N'Chyaw Tang." Unpublished memoirs.

Nhkum Bu Lu. 2016. "A Woman's Life in War and Peace." In *War and Peace in the Borderlands of Myanmar: The Kachin Ceasefire, 1994–2011*, edited by Mandy Sadan, 215–30. Copenhagen, Denmark: NIAS.

Nordstrom, Carolyn. 1997. *A Different Kind of War Story*. Philadelphia: University of Pennsylvania Press.

Oishi, Mikio. 2020. "The Resurgence of the Kachin Conflict in the 'Burmese Way to Capitalism.'" In *Managing Conflicts in a Globalizing ASEAN: Incompatibility Management through Good Governance*, edited by Mikio Oishi, 47–63. Singapore: Springer. https://doi.org/10.1007/978-981-32-9570-4_3.

Ong, Andrew. 2023. *Stalemate: Autonomy and Insurgency on the China-Myanmar Border*. Ithaca, NY: Cornell University Press.

Owens, Patricia. 2015. *Economy of Force Counterinsurgency and the Historical Rise of the Social*. Cambridge, UK: Cambridge University Press.

Parashar, Swati. 2009. "Feminist International Relations and Women Militants: Case Studies from Sri Lanka and Kashmir." *Cambridge Review of International Affairs* 22 (2): 235–56. https://doi.org/10.1080/09557570902877968.

Parashar, Swati. 2014. *Women and Militant Wars—The Politics of Injury*. London: Routledge. https://doi.org/10.1017/CBO9781107415324.004.

Persson, Alma, and Fia Sundevall. 2019. "Conscripting Women: Gender, Soldiering, and Military Service in Sweden 1965–2018." *Women's History Review* 28 (7): 1039–56. https://doi.org/10.1080/09612025.2019.1596542.

Peterson, V. Spike. 2009. "Gendering Informal Economies in Iraq." In *Women and War in the Middle East: Transnational Perspectives*, Nadje Al-Ali and Nicola Pratt, 35–64. London: Zed Books.

Peterson, V. Spike. 2010. "Gendered Identities, Ideologies, and Practices in the Context of War and Militarism." In *Gender, War, and Militarism: Feminist Perspectives*, edited by Laura Sjoberg and Sandra Via, 17–29. Westport, CT: Praeger.

Pettersson, Lena, Alma Persson, and Anders W. Berggren. 2008. "Changing Gender Relations: Women Officers' Experiences in the Swedish Armed Forces." *Economic and Industrial Democracy* 29 (2): 192–216. https://doi.org/10.1177/0143831X07088541.

Pittaway, Eileen, Linda Bartolomei, and Richard Hugman. 2010. "'Stop Stealing Our Stories': The Ethics of Research with Vulnerable Groups." *Journal of Human Rights Practice* 2 (2): 229–51. https://doi.org/10.1093/jhuman/huq004.

Project Maje. 1995. "This Revolutionary Life: Women of the Kachin Liberated Area." Cranford, NJ: Project Maje.

Rai, Shirin M., Catherine Hoskyns, and Dania Thomas. 2014. "Depletion: The Costs of Social Reproduction." *International Feminist Journal of Politics* 16 (1): 86–105.

Rajah, Ananda. 2002. "A 'Nation of Intent' in Burma: Karen Ethno-Nationalism, Nationalism and Narrations of Nation." *Pacific Review* 15 (4): 517–37. https://doi.org/10.1080/0951274021000029413.

Rajah, Ananda. 2008. *Remaining Karen: A Study of Cultural Reproduction and the Maintenance of Identity.* Canberra: Australian National University Press and Asia Pacific Press.

Ralph, Saw, and Naw Sheera. 2020. *Fifty Years in the Karen Revolution in Burma: The Soldier and the Teacher.* Ithaca, NY: Cornell University Press.

Refugees International. 2017. "Suffering in Shadows: Aid Restrictions and Reductions Endanger Displaced Persons in Northern Myanmar." Refugees International. www.refugeesinternational.org.

Revkin, Mara Redlich. 2021. "Competitive Governance and Displacement Decisions under Rebel Rule: Evidence from the Islamic State in Iraq." *Journal of Conflict Resolution* 65 (1): 46–80. https://doi.org/10.1177/0022002720951864.

Revkin, Mara Redlich, and Ariel I. Ahram. 2020. "Perspectives on the Rebel Social Contract: Exit, Voice, and Loyalty in the Islamic State in Iraq and Syria." *World Development* 132 (104981). https://doi.org/10.1016/j.worlddev.2020.104981.

Robinne, Francois, and Mandy Sadan, eds. 2007. *Social Dynamics in the Highlands of Southeast Asia: Reconsidering Political Systems of Highland Burma.* Leiden, The Netherlands: Brill.

Roy, Srila. 2006. "Revolutionary Marriage: On the Politics of Sexual Stories in Naxalbari." *Feminist Review*, no. 83, 99–118. https://www.jstor.org/stable/3874385.

Roy, Srila. 2012. *Remembering Revolution: Gender, Violence and Subjectivity in India's Naxalbari Movement.* Delhi, India: Oxford University Press.

Sadan, Mandy. 2013. *Being & Becoming Kachin: Histories beyond the State in the Borderworlds of Burma.* Oxford, UK: Oxford University Press.

Sadan, Mandy. 2014. "The Extraordinariness of Ordinary Lives." In *Burmese Lives: Ordinary Life Stories under the Burmese Regime*, edited by Wen-Chin Chang and Eric Tagliacozzo, 25–53. Oxford, UK: Oxford University Press.

Sadan, Mandy. 2015. "Ongoing Conflict in the Kachin State." *South East Asian Affairs* 6, 246–59.

Sadan, Mandy, ed. 2016. *War and Peace in the Borderlands of Myanmar: The Kachin Ceasefire, 1994–2011.* Copenhagen, Denmark: NIAS.

Sadan, Mandy. 2024. "Kachin Communities in Myanmar." In *Oxford Research Encyclopedias.* Oxford, UK: Oxford University Press.

Sadan, Mandy, and Ja Htoi Pan Maran. 2022. "Gendering Kachinland Challenging the Gender Blindness of an Ethnographic Area in Highland Asia." In *Routledge Handbook of Highland Asia*, edited by Jelle J. P. Wouters and Michael T. Heneise, 325–36. Abingdon, UK: Routledge.

Sarma, Jasnea, Alessandro Rippa, and Karin Dean. 2023. "'We Don't Eat Those Bananas': Chinese Plantation Expansions and Bordering on Northern Myanmar's Kachin Borderlands." *Eurasian Geography and Economics* 64 (7–8). https://doi.org/10.1080/15387216.2023.2215802.

Sasson-Levy, Orna. 2002. "Constructing Identities at the Margins: Masculinities and Citizenship in the Israeli Army." *Sociological Quarterly* 43 (3).

Scheper-Hughes, Nancy. 1992. *Death without Weeping: The Violence of Everyday Life in Brazil.* Berkeley: University of California Press.

Seng, Shirley. 2014. *Me and the Revolutionary Journey.* Burma Ethnic Studies (BCES). Accessed September 23, 2024. https://www.scribd.com/document/369516957/Shelly-Seng-me-and-R-journey-pdf.

Shah, Alpa. 2013. "The Intimacy of Insurgency: Beyond Coercion, Greed or Grievance in Maoist India." *Economy and Society* 42 (3): 480–506. https://doi.org/10.1080/03085147.2013.783662.

SIPRI. 2023. "SIPRI Military Expenditure Database." SIPRI. https://www.sipri.org/databases/milex.

Sjoberg, Laura. 2010. "Women Fighters and the 'Beautiful Soul' Narrative." *International Review of the Red Cross* 92 (877): 53–68.

Sjoberg, Laura. 2014. *Gender, War, and Conflict*. Cambridge, UK: Polity.

Smith, Dorothy. 1987. *The Everyday World as Problematic*. Boston: Northeastern University Press.

Smith, Martin. 1999. *Burma: Insurgency and the Politics of Ethnicity*. London: Zed Books.

Smith, Martin. 2016. "Reflections on the Kachin Ceasefire: A Cycle of Hope and Disappointment." In *War and Peace in the Borderlands of Myanmar: The Kachin Ceasefire, 1994–2011*, edited by Mandy Sadan, 57–91. Copenhagen, Denmark: NIAS.

South, Ashley. 2007. "Karen Nationalist Communities: The 'Problem' of Diversity." *Contemporary Southeast Asia* 29 (1): 55–76. https://doi.org/10.1355/CS29-1C.

South, Ashley. 2008. *Ethnic Politics in Burma: States of Conflict*. London: Routledge.

Stathis, Kalyvas. 2006. *The Logic of Violence in Civil War*. New York: Cambridge University Press.

Steinmüller, Hans. 2022. "Sovereignty as Care: Acquaintances, Mutuality, and Scale in the Wa State of Myanmar." *Comparative Studies in Society and History* 64 (4): 910–33. https://doi.org/10.1017/S0010417522000299.

Stern, Maria, and Sanna Strand. 2021. "Periods, Pregnancy, and Peeing: Leaky Feminine Bodies in Swedish Military Marketing." *International Political Sociology*, 1–21. https://doi.org/10.1093/ips/olab025.

Sylvester, Christine. 2012. *War as Experience: Contributions from International Relations and Feminist Analysis*. New York: Routledge.

Tanyag, Maria. 2024. *The Global Politics of Sexual and Reproductive Health*. Oxford, UK: Oxford University Press.

Thant Myint-U. 2019. *The Hidden History of Burma—Race, Capitalism, and the Crisis of Democracy in the 21st Century*. New York: W. W. Norton.

Tharaphi Than. 2014. *Women in Modern Burma*. London: Routledge.

Tharaphi Than, ed. 2024. *Special Issue on Feminism*. Vol. 4. Independent Journal of Burmese Scholarship 2. Chiang Mai, Thailand: Wanida Press.

Thawnghmung, Ardeth Maung. 2011. *Beyond Armed Resistance: Ethnonational Politics in Burma (Myanmar)*. Policy Studies (15471349). Honolulu: East-West Center.

Thawnghmung, Ardeth Maung. 2019. *Everyday Economic Survival in Myanmar*. Madison: University of Wisconsin Press.

Thawnghmung, Ardeth Maung, and Violet Cho. 2013. "Karen Nationalism and Armed Struggle: From the Perspective of Zipporah Sein." In *Women in Southeast Asian Nationalist Movements: A Biographical Approach*, 250–75. Singapore: National University of Singapore Press.

Thiranagama, Shakira. 2011. *In My Mother's House: Civil War in Sri Lanka*. Philadelphia: University of Pennsylvania Press.

Trisko Darden, Jessica. 2023. "Ukrainian Wartime Policy and the Construction of Women's Combatant Status." *Women's Studies International Forum* 96 (102665). https://doi.org/10.1016/j.wsif.2022.102665.

Trocaire and Oxfam. 2017. "Life on Hold: Experiences of Women Displaced by Conflict in Kachin State, Myanmar." Yangon. https://www.trocaire.org/documents/life-on-hold-experiences-of-women-displaced-by-conflict-in-kachin-state-myanmar/.

True, Jacqui. 2012. *The Political Economy of Violence against Women*. Oxford, UK: Oxford University Press.

True, Jacqui, and Maria Tanyag. 2017. "Global Violence and Security from a Gendered Perspective." In *Global Insecurity: Futures of Global Chaos and Governance*, edited by Anthony Burke and Rita Parker, 43–63. London: Palgrave Macmillan. https:// doi.org/10.1057/978-1-349-95145-1_3.

UNCHR and UNDP. 2018. "Housing, Land and Property 2018 Baseline Assessment in Kachin State."

UN Human Rights Council (UNHRC). 2023. "Report of the Independent Investigative Mechanism for Myanmar." Human Rights Situations That Require the Council's Attention. June 30. Geneva, Switzerland: Human Rights Council. https://iimm .un.org/wp-content/uploads/2023/08/G2312500.pdf.

United Nations Development Program. 2015. "The State of Local Governance: Trends in Kachin." Yangon. https://www.undp.org/myanmar/publications/state-local -governance-trends-kachin.

UNOCHA. 2021. "Humanitarian Needs Overview—Myanmar." https://www.unocha.org /publications/report/myanmar/myanmar-2021-humanitarian-needs-overview -january-2021.

UNOCHA. 2022. "Progress Made and Remaining Challenges with Regard to the Rec- ommendations of the Independent International Fact-Finding Mission on Myan- mar." https://www.ohchr.org/sites/default/files/documents/hrbodies/hrcouncil /regularsession/session51/2022-09-16/A_HRC_51_41_auv.docx.

UN Office for the Coordination of Humanitarian Affairs. 2014. "Humanitarian Response Plan 2015." Nay Pyi Taw, Republic of the Union of Myanmar.

UN Office for the Coordination of Humanitarian Affairs. 2016. "2017 Humanitarian Response Plan Myanmar." Nay Pyi Taw, Republic of the Union of Myanmar.

UN Office for the Coordination of Humanitarian Affairs. 2017. "2018 Interim Humani- tarian Response Plan." Nay Pyi Taw, Republic of the Union of Myanmar.

UN Women. 2021. "Gender Profile for Humanitarian Action: Rakhine, Kachin, North- ern Shan and Kayin States, Myanmar." June. Vol. 3. https://www.unocha.org /attachments/767664ef-6c33-3bee-a30b-0c9b1f98b385/Gender%20profile %20for%20humanitarian%20action%202021.pdf.

Vastapuu, Leena. 2018. *Liberia's Women Veterans: War, Roles and Reintegration*. London: Zed Books.

Vermeij, Lotte. 2020. "Woman First, Soldier Second: Taboos and Stigmas Facing Mili- tary Women in UN Peace Operations." International Peace Institute.

Viterna, Jocelyn. 2013. *Women in War: The Micro-Processes of Mobilization in El Salva- dor*. New York: Oxford University Press. https://doi.org/10.1093/acprof.

Wennmann, Achim. 2011. "Economic Dimensions of Armed Groups: Profiling the Financing, Costs, and Agendas and Their Implications for Mediated Engagements." *International Review of the Red Cross* 93 (882): 333–52. https://doi.org/10.1017 /S1816383111000361.

Wibben, Annick T. R. 2011. *Feminist Security Studies: A Narrative Approach. Feminist Security Studies: A Narrative Approach*. London: Taylor & Francis.

Williams, Benjamin. 2017. "Excess of Love: An Oral History of the Kachin Indepen- dence Organization." Thesis Supplement, Williams College.

Wood, Elisabeth Jean. 2006. "The Ethical Challenges of Field Research in Conflict Zones." *Qualitative Sociology* 15: 373–86.

Wood, Reed M. 2019. *Female Fighters: Why Rebel Groups Recruit Women for War*. New York: Columbia University Press. https://doi.org/10.7312/wood19298.

Wood, Reed M., and Jakana L. Thomas. 2017. "Women on the Frontline: Rebel Group Ideology and Women's Participation in Violent Rebellion." *Journal of Peace Research* 54 (1): 31–46. https://doi.org/10.1177/0022343316675025.

Woods, Kevin. 2011. "Ceasefire Capitalism: Military–Private Partnerships, Resource Concessions and Military–State Building in the Burma–China Borderlands." *Journal of Peasant Studies* 38 (4): 747–70. https://doi.org/10.1080/03066150.2011.607699.

Woodward, Rachel, and Claire Duncanson. 2016. "Gendered Divisions of Military Labour in the British Armed Forces." *Defence Studies* 16 (3): 205–28. https://doi.org/10.1080/14702436.2016.1180958.

Yuval-Davis, Nira. 1985. "Front and Rear: The Sexual Division of Labor in the Israeli Army." *Feminist Studies* 11 (3): 649–75.

Yuval-Davis, Nira. 1997. *Gender and Nation*. London: Sage.

Zharkevich, Ina. 2019. *Maoist People's War and the Revolution of Everyday Life in Nepal*. Cambridge, UK: Cambridge University Press.

Zin Mar Oo, and Kyoko Kusakabe. 2010. "Motherhood and Social Network: Response Strategies of Internally Displaced Karen Women in Taungoo District." *Women's Studies International Forum* 33 (5): 482–91. https://doi.org/10.1016/j.wsif.2010.06.006.

Index

abortion, 6, 40
Abu-Lughod, Lila, ix
abuses by military, 14, 64
"active service members," 57
addiction, 4, 5, 15, 56–57, 121n11
administrative/clerical roles, 19, 43, 50, 59, 62, 68–70, 90, 104
adolescents. *See* young people
adultery, 70
affective resources, 5, 7–8, 32, 35, 74, 94–96, 100–1, 110, 111, 116
agriculture/agricultural labor, 5, 103–5
  banana production, 6, 10, 34, 36–38, 40, 44
  commuting to work, 114
  counterinsurgency campaigns, 109
  displacement from land, 29, 31, 34–39, 111, 114
  pig farms, 1, 29, 34, 104
  political economy, 45, 51–53, 55, 57
  purchase of farm animals, 110
  regional and community development, 57
  sugar production, 6, 10, 34, 36, 38, 40
Ahmed, Sara, 17
aid, humanitarian, 4–6, 16, 33, 39, 113
air strikes, 16, 30
Akawa, Martha, 64
alcohol, vice inherent in military, 87
Al-Khalili, Charlotte, 95
All Burma Students' Democratic Front, 21
Alliance for Gender Inclusion in the Peace Process, 20
A Nang Pa massacre, 16
Andaya, Barbara Watson, 9
anxiety and stress, 30, 31, 113
"armed peace," 15
Aung San Suu Kyi, 25

"bad/corrupt women" in military, 85, 86, 91
Bamar people, 40, 79, 96
banana crops, 6, 10, 34, 36–38, 40, 44
Bangkok, 19
birth. *See* childbirth
birth certificates, 57
blindness, 29, 30
Bolivarian revolution, 107

bombings, 16, 30
border
  Chinese border, 10, 11, 30, 83, 88
  cross-border trade, 53
  Thai border, 17
Border Guard Force, 15, 16
breastfeeding, 40, 103, 104
Brenner, David, 58
British, independence from, 11, 47
brothers, sisters' military service on behalf of, 4, 63, 78, 79, 84, 85, 89
Burma
  Bamar people, 40, 79, 96
  Burmese Border Guard Forces, 15, 16
  Burmese language, 20, 59, 81
  burning of villages, 14, 36, 113

camp-in-charges, 38
camps. *See* displaced persons
caring, within militarized social reproduction, 26, 94, 110
cashier work, 105
casino work, 109, 112
ceasefire between government and KIO/KIA, 7, 14–16, 22, 56–58, 66, 82, 103–4
  breakdown. *See* new war
"ceasefire capitalism," 82
Central Commitee (CC), 19, 44, 54, 58, 59, 67, 71–73, 80, 83, 98
Chávez, Hugo, 107
Chiang Mai, Thailand, 2, 19, 50
chickens, 109
chiefs (*duwas*), 13, 99
childbirth, 4, 6, 40, 61, 65, 94
  "genocidal attacks," response to, 4
  midwifery, 48, 61
  military service, discontinuation of, 73, 90, 99
childcare/child-rearing, 2, 30, 37, 62, 102–5
  grandparents providing, 7, 94, 106
  nurseries and childcare centers, 31, 44, 55, 56, 105
children, vii, 4, 6, 16, 29, 33
  infant sickness, 34
  loss of, 40, 62
  nutritional deficits, 10